CONTEMPORARY WRITERS

General Editors
MALCOLM BRADBURY
and
CHRISTOPHER BIGSBY

# JOHN LE CARRÉ

IN THE SAME SERIES

# JOHN
# LE CARRÉ

## ERIC HOMBERGER

METHUEN
LONDON AND NEW YORK

*First published in 1986 by*
*Methuen & Co. Ltd*
*11 New Fetter Lane, London EC4P 4EE*

*Published in the USA by*
*Methuen & Co.*
*in association with Methuen, Inc.*
*29 West 35th Street, New York, NY 10001*

© *1986 Eric Homberger*

*Typeset by Rowland Phototypesetting Ltd*
*Printed in Great Britain by*
*Richard Clay (The Chaucer Press) Ltd*
*Bungay, Suffolk*

British Library Cataloguing in Publication Data

*Homberger, Eric*
*John Le Carré.—(Contemporary writers)*
*1. Le Carré, John—Criticism and*
*interpretation*
*I. Title     II. Series*
*823'.914     PR6062.E33Z/*
*ISBN 0-416-40450-2*


Library of Congress Cataloging in Publication Data

*Homberger, Eric.*
*John Le Carré*
*(Contemporary writers)*
*Bibliography: p.*
*1. Le Carré, John, 1939–   —Criticism and interpretation.*
*2. Spy stories, English—History and criticism.*
*I. Title.     II. Series.*
*PR6062.E33Z69   1986   823'.914   86-18018*
*ISBN 0-416-40450-2 (pbk.)*

# CONTENTS

# GENERAL EDITORS' PREFACE

The contemporary is a country which we all inhabit, but there is little agreement as to its boundaries or its shape. The serious writer is one of its most sensitive interpreters, but criticism is notoriously cautious in offering a response or making a judgement. Accordingly, this continuing series is an endeavour to look at some of the most important writers of our time, and the questions raised by their work. It is, in effect, an attempt to map the contemporary, to describe its aesthetic and moral topography.

The series came into existence out of two convictions. One was that, despite all the modern pressures on the writer and on literary culture, we live in a major creative time, as vigorous and alive in its distinctive way as any that went before. The other was that, though criticism itself tends to grow more theoretical and apparently indifferent to contemporary creation, there are grounds for a lively aesthetic debate. This series, which includes books written from various standpoints, is meant to provide a forum for that debate. By design, some of those who have contributed are themselves writers, willing to respond to their contemporaries; others are critics who have brought to the discussion of current writing the spirit of contemporary criticism or simply a conviction, forcibly and coherently argued, for the contemporary significance of their subjects. Our aim, as the series develops, is to continue to explore the works of major post-war writers – in fiction, drama and poetry – over an international range, and thereby to illuminate not only those works but also in some degree the artistic, social and moral assumptions on which they rest. Our wish is that, in their very variety of approach and emphasis, these books will stimulate interest in and understanding of the vitality of a living literature which, because it is contemporary, is especially ours.

*Norwich, England*                                    MALCOLM BRADBURY
                                                      CHRISTOPHER BIGSBY

# ACKNOWLEDGEMENTS

I would like to thank Giorgio Gossetti and my colleague Professor Guido Almansi, through whose good offices I was invited to participate in the Mystfest colloquium on le Carré, which was held in Cattolica, Italy, in 1985, at which I was able to try out certain thoughts on the Forsterizing of Philby. Thanks are also due to those who assisted in the writing of this book: Pippa Stewart of Hodder & Stoughton Ltd; Livia Gollancz and Richenda Todd of Victor Gollancz Ltd; Hilary Rubinstein of A. P. Watt Ltd; the Features Department of the *Sunday Telegraph Magazine*; George Greenfield of John Farquharson Ltd, who provided me with a typescript of *A Perfect Spy*; John le Carré, who kindly allowed me to read his most recent novel before publication; and Michael Straight and William Colby, who were kind enough to answer queries. The School of English and American Studies provided the shiny machine on which this manuscript was haltingly composed. The general editors of this series were helpful indeed on certain matters of prose style and argumentation. The impetus to write about le Carré was given particular focus during a paper on 'George Smiley and the Post-Imperial Neurosis' delivered by Geoffrey Hemsted of the University of Sussex at a conference at Ruskin College in 1984. I suspect that Mr Hemsted will disagree with my conclusions as comprehensively as I disagreed with his as expressed at Ruskin College.

Permission to quote short extracts from the novels of John le Carré has been granted by John Farquharson Ltd on behalf of the author.

*University of East Anglia, 1986*          ERIC HOMBERGER

# A NOTE ON THE TEXTS

Le Carré's books have been frequently reprinted. As pagination between British and American editions, both hardbound and paperback, differs, it seemed appropriate to cite the source of quotation by chapter.

It also seemed desirable in a study of this length to avoid footnotes, and to indicate in the text the source of material cited, either by author's name or by a reference to an author and date within parentheses. Interviews with le Carré are listed chronologically in the bibliography. The following abbreviations have been used:

CD      *Call for the Dead*
MQ      *A Murder of Quality*
SCC     *The Spy Who Came in From the Cold*
LGW     *The Looking-Glass War*
STG     *A Small Town in Germany*
NSL     *The Naive and Sentimental Lover*
TTSS    *Tinker, Tailor, Soldier, Spy*
HS      *The Honourable Schoolboy*
SP      *Smiley's People*
LDG     *The Little Drummer Girl*
PS      *A Perfect Spy*

# INTRODUCTION

When in 1930 F. R. Leavis published his pamphlet *Mass Civilization and Minority Culture* it seemed to some sensitive observers that the terms 'civilization' and 'culture' were virtually antithetical:

> It is not merely that the power and the sense of authority are now divorced from culture, but that some of the most disinterested solicitude for civilization is apt to be, consciously or unconsciously, inimical to culture.

Among the most telling of Leavis's examples are the mechanisms of literary distribution and publicity, such as the Book Society, Book Guild and the judgements of reviewers (the prime specimen being the weekly book column of the novelist Arnold Bennett in the *Evening Standard*), whose activities could be countenanced only in a society in which an 'informed and cultivated public' no longer existed. Half a century later the situation in some respects is scarcely better: a vast and powerful bestseller system has firmly separated what Leavis describes as 'culture' (or the fully serious) from 'civilization', which loosely stands for the imperatives of corporate publishing, and its relationship to popular taste and 'the market'. The work of John Sutherland (*Bestsellers*, 1981) shows that bestsellers today are not 'literature' in the traditional sense; such books are reviewed more as media events than as works of fiction, and their creators are not the autonomous authors of yore. Behind the great blockbusters of the past two decades (such as *The Godfather*, *Jaws* and *The Omen*) lies a coordinated manipulation of the means of cultural production. In such a system the author is one among a substantial team which puts the bestseller together: ideas must be originated and developed; editors assist with matters of plot, style and narrative technique; agents and lawyers recognize and exploit the commercial potential of the 'product'; corporate finance must be planned; subsidiary rights sold; contracts drawn up; publicity tours arranged. The current term in the USA for such works is 'pitched', that is created and sold as a commercial package. The 'writer' is usually brought into the deal at a late stage, and the author may not be the person who actually writes the book. Maureen Dean, wife of the lawyer involved in the Watergate scandal, once boasted that *Mo: One Woman's Story of Watergate*, which she 'wrote' in collaboration with Hays Gorey, was a book which she had not written nor even read.

How remote all this is from the old world of 'culture' as Leavis believed it to be. Malcolm Bradbury asserted in 1971 that 'we expect our writers to be free to appeal to their own distinctive experience, to explore their own individual terms of creativity or their own passions and impulses'. In order to be published, individual creativity passes into the hands of people and institutions with quite different priorities, people perhaps who talk about 'product' and 'the bottom line'. The bestseller system is in its very nature hostile to liberal conceptions of individual creativity and the independent imagination. Richard Hoggart argued in *The Uses of Literacy* (1957) that 'good writing cannot be popular today, and popular writing cannot genuinely explore experience'. Thirty years later there seem to be fewer defenders of 'high' culture (in the old sense), and more resigned capitulation before the almighty logic of commerce and profit. At other times the barriers between serious and popular seem as formidable, as impermeable, as though just discovered. A bestselling and therefore 'popular' writer confronts a literary establishment in Britain which is deeply suspicious, in a liberal way, of popular taste. Some of these reviewers would be as frank as Hoggart was in 1957; many more would quietly share his opinion. The result is a peculiar blend of enthusiasm and condescension which one finds in 'ghetto' reviews of detective stories, science fiction and

12

spy stories, and not a little suspicion of genre writers with literary pretensions.

John le Carré is one of the very few writers in England today who is 'popular' and 'serious'. He is reviewed with the attention of a Fowles, Golding or Greene, while successfully competing for rack space in book stores with Jeffrey Archer and James Herbert. The reasons for his success are culturally interesting. Le Carre's books contain no gang-rapes or witty transvestism; they portray no new ice age or natural disasters; his villains seem of no more than ordinary size and strength; there are no monomaniacal killer animals and no billionaires with humourless plots to take over the world. His books lack shiny technological marvels and (leaving aside *The Naive and Sentimental Lover* and *The Little Drummer Girl*) have little romance in them. The most moving relationships are either between men, such as Avery and Leiser, or between women, such as Connie Sachs and Hilary. There are no ambitious career women or dynastic family sagas, or titanic struggles for control of vast industrial empires in his books. They contain no trade unionists, cynical capitalists, sensitive investigative journalists or coppers with street smarts. None of the 'items of high civilization' which the young Henry James engagingly lists in his study of Nathaniel Hawthorne appears in le Carré's books nor, as this list suggests, does he deal in the staple ingredients of our popular fiction. With the very large exception of the Karla trilogy, in his books there isn't even a decent Russian conspiracy to take over the free world.

Le Carré is in most respects a traditional writer. John Halperin (1980) sees him as someone who is 'in many ways old-fashioned, even Victorian'. Like Jim Prideaux bemoaning the disappearance of cars like the Alvis, he regrets the decline in British fiction: 'We *used* to produce great narrative writers, and by and large we don't any more' (Heald, 1977); forty-eight volumes of the Caxton edition of Balzac are on the shelves of his study in Cornwall (Cameron, 1974). All of his books have third-person narratives. (*A Perfect Spy* largely consists of Magnus Pym's farewell letters to Jack Brotherhood and to his son, but even here he frequently writes of himself in the third person as 'Pym'.) He has sought some extraordinarily intricate plots, while retaining a clear narrative voice. To hazard a guess, since the unfortunate reception of *The Naïve and Sentimental Lover* in 1971 (see pp. 69–70) he has probably not paid much attention to contemporary experimental or post-modernist writing. He is a writer, in a slightly old-fashioned sense, for whom fiction is not a form of 'play'. As with the books of George Orwell, one has the feeling that there is an enduring moral seriousness in le Carré.

One aspect of his work which makes le Carré stand out among writers of both popular and serious fiction is his politics. As John Sutherland shows, most examples of popular fiction have *Rambo* politics, if not something sicker and more overtly fascistic. In a culture in which experimental novels tend to avoid political issues (*Ulysses*, *The Waves*, *The Sound and the Fury*), and which are often rooted in fantasies of rage and violence, le Carré is a striking exception. His books have often had layers of political implication and meaning, in an age in which impatience with 'the political' often takes the form of a condensation of the complex and the ambiguous into the simple, easily grasped symbol. Condensation is at war with the complicated, with the suspended judgements, the balanced temperament, the maturity, of our liberalism. Le Carré is not, in fact, a saintly and high-minded liberal, but a man with strong feelings and a devastating capacity to represent the self-deceptions demanded by the state. As powerfully as any writer of his generation, he has portrayed the political dilemmas of post-imperial Britain. He has not written directly about the high political issues of the day, nor about politicians. He has, rather, shown values in conflict with policies and institutions. The state and the claims it makes upon the consciences of its servants and victims are traditionally the terrain of the liberal novelist, and are le Carré's ultimate subject. It would be misleading to call him a political novelist; he is rather a novelist for whom meaningful experience and moral life are not disengaged from politics.

*

Le Carré was born David Cornwell in Poole, Dorset, in 1931, the younger son of a Nonconformist family. His grandfather, a

14

builder who rose to become Lord Mayor of Poole, maintained an environment of great piety and decorum in the family: 'We sang hymns at home every Sunday with my aunt thumping away at the harmonium' (Pitman, 1965). The marriage of his parents, Ronald and Olive (nicknamed 'Glassy') ended abruptly when his mother walked out on the family when David was 6. In *The Naive and Sentimental Lover* (1971) Shamus asks Aldo Cassidy about his mother:

> 'She left me when I was small. Seven.'
> 'You said five before.'
> 'Five then.'
> 'What effect did this have on you, Cassidy?'
> 'Well . . . it made me lonely I suppose . . . it sort of . . . robbed me of my childhood.'
> 'What does that mean?' Shamus enquired, sitting bolt upright.
> 'What?' said Cassidy.
> 'What do you mean by being *robbed of childhood*?'
> 'Denied normal growth, I suppose,' Cassidy faltered, 'a sense of fun . . . I had no female reference, no one to make women human.' (*NSL*, ch. 20)

As he wrote in a biographical statement for John Wakeman's *World Authors 1950–1970* (1975), 'I find it hard to write about women; although I can understand intellectually why they act as they do I find it difficult to imagine myself acting in that way'. Le Carré's treatment of women is discussed in Chapter 4. Betrayal, in all its protean forms, is his insistent theme.

Le Carré's father, Ronnie Cornwell, a 'Micawber character' (M. Gross, 1980), 'a charming but reckless schemer with a penchant for lying' (Behr, 1983), was certainly the most important influence upon his life. He repeatedly drew his son into his schemes. 'I was his fluent boy, his charming clown, the one who answered the phone to explain why he couldn't come to a meeting or that a cheque was in the mail' (Behr, 1983). Le Carré was sent to a succession of preparatory schools, and then to Sherborne School (where Aldo Cassidy, too, was educated), which he found 'a very pious place indeed' (Pitman, 1965). 'We were ruled by the rod, and by the athletes' (M. Gross, 1980). He stuck it until 1948, when he was allowed to attend Berne University where he studied German. Leaving Sherborne was a way to escape Ronnie. He did not learn until he was 18 that his father was a convicted felon, who had served a term in prison while David was a small boy. A Swiss university in 1948 posed new kinds of problems. 'I was there for nine months – and for the first seven I spoke to absolutely no one. I did no work. No girls. I just mooched' (Pitman, 1965). A 'retired British intelligence source' (Behr, 1983) suggests that le Carré had his first contact with the secret service while in Switzerland. The fateful meeting between Magnus Pym and Axel, friend and spymaster in *A Perfect Spy*, is set in Berne.

It was a strange, writerly sort of childhood. Betrayed by his mother, entertained, manipulated and pestered by his father, le Carré grew up the bearer of secret and dangerous knowledge about his family. As a boy he lived a secret double life, and was attracted to writers similarly obsessed with the figure of the *isolato* and the man betrayed. He often included Conrad and Greene among his favourite authors.

Le Carré did his National Service after returning from Berne in 1949. He served in the Intelligence Corps in Austria, where he worked with 'an extremely down-at-heel interrogation unit where we were trying to coax people across the Czechoslovak border and clean them of information, de-brief them' (Bragg, 1976). He belongs to the generation of English writers for whom the Cold War was their formative political experience, and has remained deeply engaged with its devastating consequences. He talks about the transition from hot war to Cold War with a still-remembered sense of the shocking rapidity of its reversals: 'It was as if the gun barrels had simply been turned in another direction' (Behr, 1983). And he remains alive to its paradoxes:

> Ever since the hot war turned into the cold war and the cold war turned into detente, we've gone through a succession of lunatic ideological reversals: people who were bombing Berlin in 1945 were running the airlift in 1948. (Bragg, 1976)

It is not quite the world of Orwell's *Nineteen Eighty-Four*, but le Carré registered the swiftness of the change as perhaps another sign of the untrustworthiness of the 'powers', of the institutions of the social order.

After leaving the army, he went up to Lincoln College, Oxford, in 1952 to study German. The ubiquitous 'intelligence source' (Behr, 1983) asserts that le Carré compiled intelligence reports on left-wing student activists while at Oxford. In *A Perfect Spy* Magnus dutifully enrolled in the demoralized ranks of the left: 'For his country, or whatever he called it, Pym addressed envelopes and memorised the addresses, played steward at public meetings, marched in dispirited processions, and afterwards wrote down whoever came' (*PS*, ch. 10). At the end of his second year, in 1954, he was forced to leave the university when his father finally was declared a bankrupt. After working for a year as an unqualified teacher at Millfield, he returned to Lincoln College on a scholarship. He married Ann Sharp and in 1956 obtained a first-class degree.

Le Carré taught German at Eton for two years, but found the atmosphere 'wholly suffocating' and isolated from the realities of modern life which he had observed in Switzerland and Austria (Cameron, 1974); he also remarked that he left Eton because he found himself involved in a 'social war', living midway 'between the drawing room and the servants' green baize door' (Pitman, 1965).

Consider le Carré's education. Preparatory school and then Sherborne; piety and snobbery. A Swiss university. The Army and then Oxford, Millfield and Eton. By the age of 27 he had had an incomparable education in the folkways of British élite institutions specifically designed to foster an imperial ruling class, precisely at the moment when the empire was collapsing around him. Le Carré told Paul Vaughan in 1979 that he belonged to virtually the last generation to have been imbued with the full force of the imperial mission:

> We really were brought up to believe that we were the best and brightest, that we'd inherited the mantle of postwar imperialism, that we were the people for whom the war had been fought and now the earth was ours and we had a great duty to run it decently.

17

After Suez it was clear that one could not talk about an 'empire' without ironic deprecation. The reality of Britain, as perceived by le Carré, was of a society which no longer afforded people of his background anything to hope for. The oft-quoted words of Connie Sachs in *Tinker, Tailor, Soldier, Spy* apply equally to le Carré's generation as to Bill Haydon's: 'Poor loves. Trained to Empire, trained to rule the waves. All gone. All taken away. Bye-bye world' (ch. 13). In a hundred years, perhaps, should students of English literature and society want to grasp the feeling of that withdrawal from the world stage, le Carré's novels will have lost none of their point. Nor will Bill Haydon, 'our latter-day Lawrence of Arabia', who dreamed of 'grand designs for restoring England to influence and greatness', have lost any of the distinctive flavour of that historical moment. The saddest people in le Carré's books are the self-deceived who still believe in England's historical mission, like Leo Harting, Fred Leiser, Jim Prideaux and Jerry Westerby. The emptiest, like de Lisle and Oliver Lacon, have no enlarging vision; they believe in nothing except the exercise of bureaucratic power. It is de Lisle who says 'I don't know what I'm defending. Or what I'm representing; who does?' (*STG*, ch. 7).

While at Eton le Carré applied for late entry into the Foreign Office. Another bureaucracy to negotiate, another complex institution. Between leaving Eton in 1956 and his first posting to the embassy in Bonn in 1958, le Carré is said to have served in MI5 under the colourful Maxwell Knight, who was responsible for the MI5 penetration of the Communist Party of Great Britain in the inter-war years. *If* le Carré had been recruited into intelligence work in Switzerland, and *if* he continued this work while at Oxford, the move to MI5 in 1956 made good sense. But le Carré has always and consistently denied that he had been a spy. Informed testimony, however, has persisted in the point. He is described as an agent in Christopher Andrew's authoritative study of the British intelligence community, and in Anthony Masters's biography of Maxwell Knight. William E. Colby, who succeeded Richard Helms as Director of Central Intelligence of the CIA, sees in le Carré's novels a clear 'operational background'. It is perhaps the kind of biographical detail which one doesn't admit, no matter how obvious it is to outsiders. The 'former British intelligence operatives' consulted by Edward Behr further state that le Carré transferred from MI5 to SIS (concerned with running agents abroad), and that he was sent on an intelligence training course at a Sarratt-like camp in Scotland where he was instructed in the full range of tradecraft.

In the summer of 1961 le Carré was sent as second secretary to the British Embassy in Bonn. He was there when the Berlin Wall was erected, and he travelled frequently between Bonn and Berlin on professional matters. The Wall, as Alec Leamas saw it in *The Spy Who Came in From the Cold*, was a 'dirty, ugly thing of breeze blocks and strands of barbed wire, lit with cheap yellow light, like the backdrop for a concentration camp. East and west of the Wall lay the unrestored part of Berlin, a half-world of ruin, drawn in two dimensions, crags of war' (ch. 1). The Wall was an important political symbol, an aggressive physical assertion of *raison d'état* and the Cold War.

While commuting from his home in Great Missenden to the Foreign Office and perhaps other locations in London he had scribbled away at a mixture of a spy story and a murder mystery. Entitled *Call for the Dead*, it was turned down by Collins before being taken on by the firm of Victor Gollancz Ltd. As a serving officer in the FO he was forced to assume a pseudonym. His publishers suggested the robust name 'Chunk Smith' (sic – a misprint for Chuck?), it being the age of Tab Hunter, Rock Hudson and Rip Torn, but he preferred a posh French-sounding name, 'le Carré' (the square) (Rogers, 1982). Subsequent explanations of the origin of his adopted name have never quite added up. In 1961 David Cornwell became John le Carré, and so he remains. A second book, *A Murder of Quality*, followed in 1962. He now regards *Call for the Dead* and *A Murder of Quality* as small novels, virtually apprentice work. It is a harsh judgement, for there are some extremely effective things in both books and they demonstrate, within the confines of what he was attempting, how genuine a talent he possessed.

With le Carré's third book, which he wrote in five months, he became a bestselling author. He originally wanted to call it *The Carcass of the Lion* (Wapshott, 1982), a dud title if there ever was one, but on his publishers' request came up with an irresistible alternative. *The Spy Who Came in From the Cold* was not an immediate runaway success. Despite the efforts of Victor Gollancz, who secured advance praise from Graham Greene ('The best spy story I have ever read') and J. B. Priestley ('Superbly constructed, with an atmosphere of chilly hell'), the book was slow in gathering momentum. It received an enthusiastic review in the July *Bookman* by Ian Maclennan, and was spotted by Gordon Grimley as an Alternative Choice for the Book Society for September. But it was not until September, several months after publication and long enough for the sales of most new novels to taper off, that the press reviews and publicity began to gain momentum. To most reviewers in 1963 it seemed less a novel than a factual report on the seedy world of the security services. Kenneth Allsop in the *Daily Mail* praised le Carré's 'dossier-like knowledge of undercover Europe' and the novel was described by Francis Iles as a 'spy story documentary' in the *Guardian*. Robert Harling in the *Sunday Times* said that it contained 'no bogus superman stuff, but what must be something like the real thing'. In *The Times Literary Supplement* its 'stamp of authenticity' was noted. Because the novel seemed so authentic, it followed that it must have been written by someone with first-hand knowledge of espionage. The mysterious identity of the author, and the coy disclaimers of Victor Gollancz, fed press speculation. *The Spy Who Came in From the Cold* enjoyed a publicity triumph. It reached the bestseller lists in late 1963 and stayed there well into the next year. Le Carré was the most widely discussed writer in Britain that autumn. It was serialized after publication in the *Sunday Express*, and when it was published in the USA it sold 70,000 copies in two weeks. The film rights were snapped up; Burt Lancaster was set to play Alec Leamas. The success of the book is a case study in the bestseller system as it was in the 1960s.

Le Carré resigned from the Foreign Office in 1964. *The Spy* had won the British Crime Novel award, and shared the rather more prestigious Somerset Maugham award with Dan Jacobson. His relations with Victor Gollancz did not survive the success of his book, and le Carré signed a contract with William

Heinemann. Victor Gollancz issued ringing statements to the press about 'the le Carré affair', but the issue was never publicly explained. Le Carré took his family to live in Crete, where he wrote *The Looking-Glass War*. Paperback rights were sold to Pan for £50,000 before publication, an extremely large sum in the early 1960s. Le Carré very quickly became a wealthy man. There were probably fewer than a dozen living English writers who could command such an advance. Martin Ritt's tense production of *The Spy Who Came in From the Cold*, starring Richard Burton, Claire Bloom and Oskar Werner, appeared in 1965, and a fourth novel, *A Small Town in Germany*, appeared in 1968.

In 1971 le Carré abandoned spy novels for a picaresque romance, *The Naive and Sentimental Lover*, in which he portrayed at several removes his relationship with Susan and James Kennaway. He met the Kennaways when he moved from Crete to Vienna in 1965. The relationship between the two writers appears, suitably disguised, in le Carré's novel, and in Kennaway's *Some Gorgeous Accident* (1967). He dedicated *A Small Town in Germany* to Kennaway. Le Carré's biographers may, someday, be able to say something about the relationship and its consequences. The story has been told fragmentarily in the posthumous *Kennaway Papers* which Susan Kennaway edited in 1981. It reinforces one's sense that le Carré, perhaps more than is generally understood, sought to use personal experiences directly in his novels. It would be remarkable if he had not done so. *The Naive and Sentimental Lover* received a scathing press, but was a more interesting failure than the critics have allowed. Le Carré was divorced in 1971, and married Jane Eustace, an editor with his new publishers Hodder & Stoughton.

George Smiley was retrieved for le Carré's next book. He had appeared in *Call for the Dead* and *A Murder of Quality*, but had only very minor roles in *The Spy Who Came in From the Cold* and *The Looking-Glass War*. There was considerable speculation about whether Smiley was based upon an actual person. Sir Maurice Oldfield, the portly former Director of the Secret Intelligence Service (MI6), has been offered several times as le Carré's model. He invited Alec Guinness and Sir Maurice to lunch when the television production of *Tinker, Tailor* was being planned, perhaps to help with the characterization, but pointed out in a letter to *The Times* in 1981 that Smiley was created long before he had ever met Sir Maurice. It has also been hinted that Smiley was in part based on the writer John Bingham (Lord Clanmorris), a friend of le Carré's, and that Smiley plays a role very similar to Sir Dick White, Director-General of MI5 from 1953 to 1956. Sir Dick was one of the earliest to suspect Philby of treachery. The name is not uncommon: David Smiley of SOE parachuted into Albania during the war, and published a highly regarded memoir, *Albanian Assignment*, in 1984. Le Carré told Joseph Lelyveld in 1986 that someone he knew in the Ministry of Defence suggested Smiley's appearance, and that his long-suffering manner was based upon an old tutor at Oxford.

The return to Smiley was a decisive one in le Carré's career as a writer. The reception of *The Naive and Sentimental Lover* in 1971 must have shaken his confidence to the roots. Smiley was a strong, familiar character, a 'proxy father figure' for the novelist (*Sunday Times*, 16 March 1986). He later revealed that he conceived of the struggle between Smiley and the Russian spymaster Karla taking place across a trilogy of novels, but for cautious commercial reasons kept the larger plan to himself. *Tinker, Tailor, Soldier, Spy* appeared in 1974, *The Honourable Schoolboy* in 1977 and, two years later, *Smiley's People*. The three novels were published in a single volume edition as *The Quest for Karla* in 1982. The very remarkable BBC production of *Tinker, Tailor*, directed by John Irvin and produced by Jonathan Powell, appeared in 1979. It was perhaps the finest serialization ever to be made for British television. The books had been individually successful, but the television serial made their author virtually a household name in England. And le Carré was, by the late 1970s, reviewed with the contentiousness, and also perhaps the respect, re-served for 'serious' writers. Very high claims were made for his novels as 'serious' literature. (They were also subject to some brutally dismissive notices, mainly by England-based reviewers writing for American periodicals: of these the most important nay-sayers were Anthony Burgess and Clive James.)

After the completion of *Tinker, Tailor*, le Carré travelled extensively in the Far East. The American presence in Vietnam was in its bitter, terminal state and he may have sensed that it might provide a backdrop for the second act of the duel between Smiley and Karla. He thought that the third act might be played out in the Middle East, and travelled to Lebanon, Jordan and Israel after the publication of *The Honourable Schoolboy*. He spent several nights in conversation with Arafat, and was introduced to Shlomo Gazit, Director of Israeli Military Intelligence, who is an admirer of le Carré's books. Arafat's opinion of le Carré, and of western spy thrillers, is not known. The right plot for Smiley proved difficult to find, and in *Smiley's People* the scene returned to northern Europe for the conclusion of the trilogy.

*The Little Drummer Girl* appeared in 1983. The Arab–Israeli conflict was and is a minefield which novelists of faint heart have avoided. It had not previously been the subject for serious fiction in England. In the event, le Carré's novel became a stunning bestseller. His American publishers, Alfred A. Knopf, sold 59,000 copies on a single day in March 1983, the largest single daily sale in the firm's history. He was accused of being a 'PLO propagandist' and of having a 'pro-Palestinian line' (Walter Laqueur in *Commentary*). David Pryce-Jones in *New Republic* saw in the book le Carré's belief that 'the Palestinians are good, the Israelis are bad'. Of course nothing of the kind is true. As most reviewers noticed, and as David Monaghan has shown in his study of le Carré (1985), the book was written by someone who attempted to grasp the entire murderous tragedy of the Middle Eastern conflict. The guard dogs of the opposing sides may bark, but a careful reading of the novel reveals its fundamental generosity of spirit – a commodity in short supply in the Middle East. Le Carré has criticized the policies of the Begin government, and condemned the Israeli invasion of Lebanon with singular forthrightness: 'The attack was a monstrosity', he wrote in the *Observer* of 13 June 1982, 'launched on speciously assembled grounds, against a people who on the Israelis' own admission constitute no serious military threat.' There has been since the 1960s an ill-tempered conservative disapproval of le Carré, one perhaps more truly merited than the left-wing grumbling of Christopher Hitchins. Le Carré said in 1982 that he has always voted socialist (M. Gross), and that he would 'rather have the Russians than Trident in Cornwall' (Wapshott, 1982). His name was prominently displayed in advertisements on behalf of the nuclear freeze campaign in 1985.

*A Perfect Spy* appeared in 1986. His most autobiographical novel, and also a strikingly funny, even gleeful book from a novelist sometimes criticized for his gloomy and depressing tone, this is the first time he has been able to write directly about his father. Le Carré accompanied the publication of the novel with a remarkable article in the *Sunday Times*, 16 March 1986, in which he discussed in detail his relationship with Ronnie Cornwell. He had, as we have noticed, mentioned to several interviewers that he had had a difficult childhood. He now offers as a full-scale interpretation of his life as a writer his struggle against his father. It will clearly strengthen the tendency to read le Carré's works biographically. But I wonder whether such a titanic inner drama, such a myth of entrapment and liberation, should not await the appearance of a biography of the writer. It is too simple by half to take such a meaning as it has been provided. And so I have resisted the temptation to rewrite this book in its considerable light. It is perhaps enough, with the book riding high on bestseller charts, to suggest that it very largely fits into the developing pattern of his fiction. The reception of *A Perfect Spy* largely confirms that le Carré is a writer in every sense worthy of 'serious' attention. His 'popular' readership will not need persuading.

# 1

## SPIES AND SPY STORIES

When the senior KGB officer Vitali Yurchenko 'defected' to the Americans in 1985, it was rather ironically pointed out that Yurchenko was the greatest coup for western intelligence since Karla went over to the British in the late 1970s. The Yurchenko affair seemed particularly le Carréan, complex, subtle and devious. When the Russian walked out on his American minders during lunch one afternoon and strolled into the Soviet Embassy in Washington, life was doing its level best to imitate art. If Yurchenko was a 'fake' defector on an operation against the CIA, Alec Leamas in *The Spy Who Came in From the Cold*, another such fake defector, showed us how meticulous such a plan had to be, and how devastating an effect it could have on the other side. The fake defector was a riskier operation than the long-term penetration agent, the 'mole': all that was required of Bill Haydon in *Tinker, Tailor, Soldier, Spy* was that he remain in character, while Leamas had to invent a 'legend', a grievance and a disintegration, which would have been quickly exposed if any detail was wrong. The intelligence war now being conducted between the KGB and their eastern friends, and the CIA, MI5, DGSE, Mossad, NSA, and so on, is a kind of ultimate chess game in which all of the moves are well-established and are studied with inordinate care. Spy stories themselves are combed for new and potentially useful twists. Dino de Laurentiis' film, *Three Days of the Condor* (1975), shows a research agency within the CIA which analysed spy stories from everywhere in the world. The head of Israeli Military Intelligence once said that the books of John le Carré were virtual textbooks for their agents. (There must have

been some interesting sessions on *The Little Drummer Girl*.)
As is well-known, real spies have written quite a few spy stories.
And, like the Mafia, whose opinions of Mario Puzo's *The
Godfather* and the films made from the novel are not without a
certain professional interest, spies have occasionally com-
mented on their fictional counterparts. Gordon Lonsdale, a
Soviet 'illegal' (an agent with a false identity working outside
the official body of accredited Soviet diplomats in the west)
who was sentenced to twenty-five years imprisonment in 1961
for his role in the Portland spy case, bemusedly noted in his
memoirs that he had not had 'passionate leave' in the manner
of James Bond after completing his assignment. Sir William
Stephenson, wartime head of the British Security Coordination
agency in North America, advised Ian Fleming, who had
worked as his subordinate during the war, that *Casino Royale*
couldn't be a success: 'It will never sell, Ian. Truth is always less
believable'. Richard Helms, who rose through the ranks to the
very top jobs within the CIA, was once interrogated over
dinner by Senator Eugene McCarthy: what was the wine
served with dinner? The sauce on one of the dishes? The name
of the flowers in the table centrepiece? When Helms admitted
that he didn't know, the senator, then urging Senate oversight
of the CIA, slyly remarked that James Bond would have done
better. Ironically, Helms, like many men in Washington,
admired Fleming's novels. He gave E. Howard Hunt formal
Agency permission to write spy thrillers, hoping perhaps that
he might prove to be an American Fleming. Before his arrest
and imprisonment over the Watergate break-in, Hunt wrote
more than forty spy stories under a variety of pseudonyms. The
spymaster Allen Dulles firmly believed that the right kind of
spy story could strengthen popular support for the Agency. He
sometimes passed on suggestions for plots to no doubt grateful
thriller writers.

It would be hard to imagine the novels of John le Carré
receiving such exalted patronage from within MI5 or MI6. He
has done more than any writer of spy stories in Britain in this
century to hold the security services up to public ridicule. 'You
*bastard*. You utter bastard', was the way le Carré was greeted
by a middle-aged intelligence officer, once a colleague, at a

diplomatic dinner at a British Embassy (*Sunday Times*, 23 March 1986). Arguably he has done what no previous writer of spy stories has done, by taking the small world of spies and making it stand, in all of its moral seediness, for the state of British society. He began working within the territory of genre fiction, and in mid-career has been recognized as a major creative presence. We do not need a literary top-of-the-pops to recognize the stature of le Carré and his importance in contemporary fiction. He is one of the very few English writers of his generation to command a large readership in the USA, despite his many hostile presentations of the 'Cousins' in the CIA, an attitude, by all accounts, warmly reciprocated. Richard Helms disliked *The Spy Who Came in From the Cold* for its mood of defeat, disillusionment and betrayal. An organization (in Helms's view) which deceived its own agents, as Leamas was deceived, soon destroyed the trust needed to maintain an intelligence service. Helms's son Dennis said that his father didn't just dislike le Carré's book, he *detested* it. Leamas understood the need for betrayal: there were solid reasons for saving the fascistic Mundt and destroying the 'good' communist Fiedler. That was the price which had to be paid, Leamas angrily explained to Liz Gold, to enable 'the great moronic mass' to sleep soundly in their beds at night. The belief-system of espionage and betrayal was left intact at the end of the book. What was so uncomfortable was that the human cost of that act of betrayal had been stripped of sanctimoniousness. It was a desolating and inhuman cost. Le Carré's novel was simply too honest for the likes of Richard Helms.

For somewhat different reasons Kim Philby also disliked *The Spy*:

> *The Spy* is very disappointing [he wrote to his wife Eleanor in 1963]. It was a relief to read a somewhat sophisticated spy-story after all that James Bond idiocy, and there are some well-thought out passages. But the whole plot from beginning to end is basically implausible, and the implausibility keeps on obtruding itself – at any rate, to anyone who has any real knowledge of the business! (E. Philby, 1968)

That Leamas was a fake defector, that Haydon might be a Russian mole, or, for that matter, that Philby himself was a double agent, seemed no less implausible. In the grey world of espionage the yardstick of 'plausibility' was itself problematic.

There are aspects of espionage which are extraordinarily subtle, devious and artful. The skills required for deception, disguise, for the artistic feigning of reality, demonstrate imagination at a high level. Many intelligent and literate people in the west have been attracted by intelligence work – on both sides, theirs and ours. Christopher Andrew noted the irony that the Russians began recruiting at Cambridge several years before MI5. The same is undoubtedly true of Harvard and the City College of New York. On the other hand, the most effective spies seem to be people like Philby and Leopold Trepper, little more than functionaries: their gift lay in a mediocrity which made them virtually invisible. The particular imaginative arts required for espionage may explain the many cases of spies being tempted to transform the fictions of their work into full-blown (or half-cocked) novels. The romantic novelist A. E. W. Mason, author of *The Four Feathers* (1902), served under Admiral Sir Reginald Hall in naval intelligence during the First World War. Mason sailed around the Mediterranean in 1915 and 1916, posing in the Ashenden manner as a rich yachtsman seeking diversion from the war. He later used some of his adventures in his books. Somerset Maugham had similar experiences and, as we shall see, gave spy fiction a more realistic literary demeanour. The ethos of the gentlemanly amateur still prevailed in the secret service of their day but, as Christopher Andrew has pointed out (1985), the practice of spying became less and less amenable to amateurs and gentleman novelists. Sophisticated techniques of decoding raised 'elint' and 'sigint' (electronic and signals intelligence) over the sadly named 'humint'. The lonely vigil of Richard Sorge in the German Embassy in Tokyo, passing on to Moscow the details of the German plans to invade the USSR in June 1941, inevitably captures the imagination. (Leopold Trepper sent the exact number of divisions which the German army high command planned to send east for the invasion, full details of the plan of attack and the final date for the invasion to his Soviet superiors, but his intelligence reports were assumed to be based upon forged German or British documents. As ever, the analysis and not the collection of intelligence was the most vulnerable stage in the process.) But the future of spying was at Bletchley Park with the codebreakers, and not with the butler with a Minox camera silently entering the minister's study. Spying lost some of its romantic appeal as it increasingly became technological and bureacratic. It took a long time for the romance to disappear from spy novels. In a sense, it remains an intensely romantic activity still.

Writers have been attracted to the figure of the spy, perhaps because as le Carré has suggested, there is a correspondence at a deeper level between the view of the world of spy and writer. They are both of necessity solitaries, obliged to keep others at a distance while extracting from them the 'material' for their work. It is this which the spy 'sells' to his or her clients and which the writer 'packages' for his readers. The writer-spy is forced to seek anonymity, while passing back and forth unobserved. '"'E's a spy", Mr Savory added,' in Graham Greene's *Stamboul Train* (1932): '"'E 'as to see everything and pass unnoticed. If people recognized 'im they wouldn't talk, they'd pose before 'im; 'e wouldn't find things out"' (pt II, ch. 1). The writer like the spy knows that nothing is ever quite what it seems. Novelists must, like spies, accept the role of 'committed doubter', as le Carré once characterized Smiley (Bragg, 1976), and function with the suspicion that we can never be quite sure we can trust those upon whom we must depend. The spy is an artist, a practitioner of deep artifice, strategem and contrivance. His triumph is ultimately a successful performance. So, too, the artist is a spy, a secret sharer, committed to the discovery and betrayal of our deepest secrets.

Throughout most of its brief history the spy story has been a lowly, hysterical, rather nasty variety of the popular thriller. It was born of the spy hysteria in Edwardian England, and used by ambitious press barons, brass hats and politicians to scare the reading public and thus to win support for increased expenditure on imperial defence. Erskine Childers's *The Riddle of the Sands* (1903) appeared against the background of a growing threat of German naval power. The book ends with an epilogue, discussing the military implications and feasibility of the German plan, and a postscript, dated March 1903, welcoming several signs of increased public awareness of the German threat. This is not clever fictionality, in the post-modernist sense, but a writer in desperate earnestness record-ing some signs that his message has begun to get through to politicians and the public. The ingenuity and plausibility of the plot, which showed that a fleet of small vessels could carry a German invasion force across the North Sea, had not in fact escaped the notice of German military planners. A similar scheme for a small boat invasion had been considered by the Germans in 1897, but was abandoned, as Paul Kennedy (1981) has shown in his fascinating note on the context of Childers's novel, in favour of the ambitious shipbuilding programme of Tirpitz. Childers was warning of a danger which, even when he was writing, had begun to recede into the past and to be replaced by something altogether more ominous from a British point of view. But the vividness of the narrative prompted the Admiralty to request a staff investigation of the dangers of an invasion along the lines suggested by Childers.

The lonely adventures of Davies and Carruthers became something of a model for the amateur spies of the Edwardian era. When two British naval officers were arrested in the Frisian islands for spying in 1910, they had a copy of Childers's novel with them, and said that it was an essential part of their equip-ment. It was not the last time when spies and spy novels were so closely linked together. Childers's book has become a naval classic, a 'yachtsman's Bible'. The description of navigating a small boat in difficult waters is so well done that its other quali-ties have been lost to view. It is a book about the amateur spirit, and is imbued with the games-playing, patriotic ethos of the public schools. The heroes are above all gentlemen, and the her-oine, Clara, steps right out of the romantic fiction of the day:

> 'Clara!' said Davies, 'will not you trust us?'
> I heard a little gasp from her. There was a flutter of lace and cambric and she was in his arms, sobbing like a tired child, her little white feet between his great clumsy sea-boots – her rose-brown cheek on his rough jersey. (ch. 28)

The 'education' of the Foreign Office clerk Carruthers follows thoroughly conventional lines. What is memorable about *The Riddle of the Sands* is the author's relaxed comfort within the literary conventions of the novel (while showing, at the same time, a near-paranoid apprehension of German plots and deviousness): there is no hint of self-conscious irony or self-parody in the narration, no doubts about the values or character of Englishness as Childers represents it. *The Riddle of the Sands* is, like the ethos it describes, a splendid example of literary amateurism.

In the wake of Childers's success other writers, more narrowly professional, rushed in to satisfy the public's growing enthusiasm for spy stories. The most prolific of these was undoubtedly William Le Queux, whose account of a German attack on England, *The Invasion of 1910*, made a sensational impact when it was first serialized in Alfred Harmsworth's *Daily Mail* in 1905. He soon acquired the reputation of being someone who knew a great deal about spying. When Major James Edmunds became head of the Special Section (later renamed MO5) of the Directorate of Military Operations in the War Office, where he found that his staff consisted of a fellow officer and a retired police detective, Edmunds turned to his friend Le Queux for current information on the German spy menace. Le Queux's books were a heady mixture of fantasy, political conspiracy and downright villainy and, with E. Phillips Oppenheim and 'Sapper', long reigned supreme at the popular end of the market. Le Carré described them both as 'talentless posturers' (*Sunday Times*, 23 March 1986).

The spy thriller was quick to establish its basic conventions. Over the years the procedures of the spy story have remained remarkably tenacious. Conventions established by the 1920s survived well into the age of Ian Fleming. They survive today, appropriately modernized, because they convey a certain kind of reading experience. Such books do not have to be well written, or to show subtleties of characterization or plot, but they must be exciting, tell a story which is capable of sustaining the interest of a mass readership and convey knowledge of things customarily hidden from public scrutiny. The literary conventions of all forms of popular writing – the plots, tricks of

31

characterization and techniques of narratives – are essentially devices for the mass-production of literature. The formulae serve to establish interchangeable novelist components which greatly reduce the complexity of writing genre fiction. The components can be ideological as well as technical, ways of seeing and understanding as well as devices of narrative and description. Such formulae also had an important meaning for readers of spy stories, and of many other kinds of popular fiction. They drastically simplified the act of reading, no less than the business of literary production. The conventions governing the appearance, behaviour and values of hero and villain, the twists and turns of the plot and the ending served to remove uncertainty from the transaction between reader and writer, and became as clearly established as those which govern popular romantic novels. So rigid were the conventions of the formulae genre that Umberto Eco in a memorable essay in 1965 described the plots of the James Bond novels as 'a machine that functions basically on a set of precise units governed by rigorous combinational rules'.

Much of what has been written on spy stories and thrillers generally has followed Eco's view that what should interest us in such works is the structuring, the mechanism, of their procedures. The other major trend in the interpretation of popular culture regarded such books as bearers of ideological messages which were themselves generated by the current state of society. All of this was, marginally, an improvement on the moralistic way that thrillers were written about a generation ago. It is hard to recall the real fervour with which writers like Dorothy L. Sayers were once praised ('definitely among the great writers' – *Observer*) and condemned. Defenders of serious cultural values like Q. D. Leavis (who described Sayers as 'odious', 'nauseating' and 'vicious' in a memorable *Scrutiny* review), and an unlikely companion, Raymond Chandler (who described Sayers's *Gaudy Night* as 'sycophantic drivel') re-garded the evident enthusiasm for detective stories as a cultural drag which threatened the fate of literature itself. Nicolas Freeling, one of the contemporary masters of the detective story, once referred to the Bond books as 'a vulgar romp for the retarded'. We are today more likely to find a value-free, technologico-criticism being written about thrillers (see Merry, 1977). They scarcely seem worth attacking with the energies of Edmund Wilson's famous diatribes, and literary criticism today has no serious vocabulary of praise. As will be clear from what follows, I have not found very much nourishment in what has been written about spy stories, and have sought my own way to read le Carré.

John Buchan, the most expert of the writers of spy thrillers, followed closely on the example of Childers. *The Thirty Nine Steps* (1915), hurriedly written in the first four months after war broke out in August 1914, describes the foiling of a German plot to obtain secret intelligence by the impersonation of a senior military figure. The book is above all an adventure story, with approximately the same kind of 'love interest' as Childers was compelled to introduce at the behest of his publishers. The politics of Buchan's novel are conservative and perfunctory. Buchan is incurious about the mentality of spies, or indeed in the mentality of any of his characters. He is more comfortable with moral categories: evil is assumed (Buchan's father was a Free Church minister and he was raised in the strictest Calvinism) and may be identified by the act of 'reading' a man or, less frequently, a woman. As Carruthers and Davies learned to 'read' Dollmann, the English traitor who was behind the invasion plot in Childers's novel, so, for Buchan, the reading of a person is basic to effective intelligence work. A person's look, dress, accent or manners provide essential evidence of character: such details serve as signs of the person's essential nature. The high arts revealed in the mastery of disguise and deception, the playing of roles and creating characters, suggest to Buchan the fundamentally theatrical nature of the undercover side of espionage. Hannay's gifts are displayed in the decoding, at a simple level, of the appearance of those he meets. When he comes across a fly-fisherman in 'deep Berkshire', Hannay sums up the man: 'I stood up and looked at him, at the square, cleft jaw and the firm folds of the cheek, and began to think that here at last was an ally worth having. His whimsical blue eyes seemed to go very deep' (ch. 7).

Inevitably villains are betrayed by some slight flaw in performance, appearance or costume. There is in Buchan a *mystique* of Englishness, and a firm belief that foreigners could never successfully counterfeit its essential quality. The crewman on the *Ariadne* gives himself away when Hannay notes his close-cropped hair, and the 'cut' of a collar and tie which would never have been worn by a true Englishman. A slight gesture by one of the bridge-players, a nervous tapping of fingers, reveals 'cruelty and ruthlessness' to Hannay in someone who appeared to be politely amiable. Buchan's racism and his fervent imperialism soon dated, especially for the young writers of the inter-war years like Greene and Ambler, but the adventures which the book puts Hannay through, and the art of reading the seemingly innocent, remained enduring elements in the genre.

The first spy story with something like a serious claim to literary merit is Somerset Maugham's *Ashenden, or: The British Agent* (1928), a collection of sixteen stories based on the author's experiences as a British agent in Switzerland and Russia during the First World War. (Le Carré regards him as by all accounts a singularly feeble and self-dramatizing agent.) It is to *Ashenden* that subsequent writers turned for an image of the moral ambiguity of espionage. Maugham was more influential in steering the spy story away from rumbustious adventure, in the manner of Buchan, and towards a subtler attention to the psychological nuances of intelligence work, than establishing the episodic short story form as the principal medium for spy stories. Ambler was strongly influenced by the *Ashenden* ethos. John le Carré told Maugham's biographer Ted Morgan that Maugham was 'the first person to write about espionage in a mood of disenchantment and [with an] almost prosaic reality' (Morgan, 1980).

The exciting adventures of a Richard Hannay or a Captain Bulldog Drummond, and the romantic fascination of spies of the First World War such as Mata Hari, gave Maugham something consciously to write against. By making his hero a sedate, middle-aged man-of-letters, Maugham broke completely with precedent: it was to Ashenden that we owe Smiley. Ashenden did not play a lone hand (this, too, was new). He knows that he is but a minor cog in a big machine, and that he can know only fragments of the truth about his assignments.

He files reports, perhaps guessing at the fate of those he deals with, but seldom has the chance to know the full truth. He has a healthy scepticism for those above him in the hierarchy, though unlike Len Deighton's Harry Palmer, that distance was not accentuated by class. Ashenden belongs to the upper bourgeoisie, and shares a wide range of attitudes (towards foreigners, women, workers, manners, and so on) which are assumed by Maugham to be commonplaces. When Ashenden comes into contact with exotic spies, such as Carmona, with his painted finger-nails, silk pyjamas and endless supplies of wigs, it is as though he had accidentally entered the terrain of Le Queux or 'Sapper'. The originality of Maugham may be seen even more clearly in his portrayal of evil. When Scudder in Buchan's *The Thirty Nine Steps* reveals the 'real boss' behind the polite facade of power ('a little white-faced Jew in a bath-chair with an eye like a rattlesnake' (ch. 1)), the author seeks to shock his readers, to make them fear and hate. Maugham rather teaches his readers to pity and despise those who have done evil things. The enemy in his book was more likely to be banal and pathetic than demonic. Espionage in *Ashenden* is stripped of glamour and romantic appeal.

The finest story in *Ashenden* concerns Grantly Caypor, an Englishman living in Switzerland who is suspected of spying for the Germans. The story follows the curve of understanding, from Ashenden's initial theorizing ('Was Caypor a good man who loved evil or a bad man who loved good?') to a more complex and despiriting perception that it is weakness and fantasy, not malign deviousness, which stands behind Caypor's air of light-hearted, bold, devil-may-care patriotism. Ashenden sees Caypor as a man who was too weak to tell his German wife that his paymasters were forcing him to return to England to continue his spying. On their last meeting Ashenden registers the fear on Caypor's face. After his departure for England, carefully arranged by British intelligence, Ashenden read doubt, terror and misery on the face of Caypor's wife. Ashenden, who had set the whole thing up, readily imagines the spy's death by firing party. Maugham ends the story on a typically Chekhovian note. He has learned to read Caypor, and the message is bleak. Ashenden was concerned to understand the psychology of those whom he must unmask and foil. Buchan took not the slightest notice of the motives of those involved in espionage. Anthony Curtis once said (1974) that for Maugham 'the psychology of a bore was always more important than the rationale behind a revolution'. Ashenden, like Smiley, made the process of understanding, the immersion in the mentality of his opponent, the central drama of effective counter-espionage.

The inter-war years were a golden age of espionage. After the peace conference at Versailles, Europe was an ant-hill of nationalist sentiment and minorities chafing under the successor regimes. The Hohenzollerns, Habsburgs and Romanovs had been swept aside, but old rivalries and old bitterness encouraged fears of plots and spying. The whole continent crawled with spies. It seemed as though every departure of the Orient Express, each luxury transatlantic liner, closed touring car, gentleman in tuxedo and dark alley in Europe were part of the *mise-en-scène* of a spy thriller. Despite Maugham, the spy was still a romantic figure in the popular imagination. In the thrillers of 'Sapper' and in Hollywood films the spy is a gentleman-hero who operates alone, confronting his opponents with quick wits and even quicker repartee. While the official security services doze, and the police are yet again shown to be bumbling and ineffective, the individual spy-hero stands between society and chaos. (Which gives a particular piquancy to the espionage activities of Christopher Isherwood's Arthur Norris, the spy-as-comic-pervert-and-fraud in *Mr Norris Changes Trains* (1935).) The legacy of Buchan and 'Sapper' pervades the spy thrillers of the 1930s, but it is Buchan harnessed to a different world-view. 'An early hero of mine', wrote Graham Greene in 1980,

> was John Buchan, but when I reopened his books [in the mid-1930s] I found I could no longer get the same pleasure from the adventures of Richard Hannay. More than the dialogue and situation had dated: the moral climate was no longer that of my boyhood. Patriotism had lost its appeal, even for a schoolboy, at Passchendaele, and the Empire brought first to mind the Beaverbrook Crusaders, while it

was difficult, during the years of Depression, to believe in the high purposes of the City of London or of the British Constitution. The hunger marchers seemed more real than the politicians. It was no longer a Buchan world. (*Ways of Escape*, p. 72)

At the outset of his career Ambler made an equally significant assessment of the spy thriller as it was in the 1930s, noting that 'Sapper' was still writing right-wing thrillers. 'He was an outright fascist. He even had his heroes dressed in black shirts. Buchan was an establishment figure, so club and fuddy-duddy, and I decided to turn that upside down and make the heroes left-wing and popular-front figures' (Laqueur, 1983).

The spirit of the post-war world showed itself in the amoral industrialists whose activities did so much to make war possible. In 1928 Ezra Pound suggested that the life of the arms dealer Sir Basil Zaharoff would make 'a fascinating document' and in the *Cantos* 'Zenos Metevsky' stands for the wickedness of the arms trade. Earnest young intellectuals like Philip Noel-Baker spent years uncovering the *Hawkers of Death* (1934) and wrote great tomes on *The Private Manufacture of Armaments* (2 vols, 1936). Though the Royal Commission which investigated the problem in 1935 was ignored, the activities of Zaharoff and the fictional versions of the corrupting capitalist became a central strand in 1930s demonology. Balterghen in Eric Ambler's *Background to Danger* (1937) was perhaps a typical figure.

Greene and Ambler wrote with a darkening sense of war hanging over Europe. As Raven in Greene's *A Gun for Sale* (1936) walks through the streets of London the newspapers warn of 'Europe Mobilizing' and of 'Ultimatums' issued. In Nottwich (Nottingham) air raid precautions were visible everywhere, and enabled Raven to gain access to his target, an evil industrialist. The atmosphere of crisis helped the younger writers of spy stories to break with the chauvinism of Buchan. *It was no longer a Buchan world.* The central figure in Greene's *The Confidential Agent* (1939) is a Spanish Republican on a mission into Baldwin's and Chamberlain's England: it seems to him a remote and exotic place, untouched by the war and death he has left behind. Kenton in *Background to Danger* forms a pragmatic alliance with a team of Soviet agents to foil a Nazi plot. One of his villains, Captain Mailler, was a former Black-and-Tan, a professional strike-breaker who is wanted for murdering a 'nigger' in the USA.

The traditional character of the agent, the forms of heroism and even the patriotic frame of reference begin to dissolve in the 1930s thrillers. Those who a decade earlier might have been heroic figures, after the model of Bulldog Drummond, now appear as bullies, womanizers, fantasists and protofascists (Buddy Ferguson in *A Gun for Sale*). The whole of Ambler's work in the 1930s is a sustained demonstration that the politics of the likes of Oppenheim and Buchan, and their two-fisted heroes, were not necessary to the spy thriller. He explained in his autobiography *Here Lies* (1985) that the traditional villains had largely lost plausibility for him in the era of Hitler:

> Power-crazed or coldly sane, master criminals or old-fashioned professional devils, I no longer believed a word of them. Nor did I believe in their passions for evil and plots against civilization. As for their world conspiracies, they appeared to me no more than toy characters rattling about inside dried peas. (ch. 7)

For Ambler the hero, who was often a fugitive, needed only an 'abysmal stupidity', which got him into interesting difficulties in the first place, 'combined with superhuman resourcefulness and unbreakable knuckle bones'. After the appearance in 1937 of his first book, *The Dark Frontier*, with its extremely unusual use of esoteric knowledge about the possibility of an atomic bomb (he had trained as an electrical engineer), Ambler was advised by the novelist Eileen Bigland to use Somerset Maugham, and particularly *Ashenden*, as a model. Ambler's first books were probably closer in technique to Buchan than to Maugham, with his thriller apparatus of physical violence, dramatic pursuits, imprisonment and escapes. But it was all coloured by a quite different spirit. Kenton's defiant words to Mailler belonged to the world of the Popular Front, with its own reversal of the good—evil simplicities of a Buchan thriller:

It's not just a struggle between Fascism and Communism, or between any other '-isms'. It's between the free human spirit and the stupid, fumbling, brutish forces of the primeval swamp. (ch. 7)

Ambler's political speeches seem rather half-hearted (they were as carefully attuned to the spirit of the age as Buchan's wartime cult of Englishness), but the idea that it might be possible to turn the politics of the spy thriller upside down, to give it a left-wing slant, represented an important extension of the genre itself.

The Second World War revolutionized the practice of intelligence work, and marked the supercession of 'humint' by 'sigint' (see p. 28). The post-war political settlement, the Europe of Yalta and the Iron Curtain, gave the spy thriller a Manichean simplicity. Unlike the inter-war years, there was a burden of actual spy cases of unprecedented public concern during the Cold War. The Rosenberg case, in particular, offered a terrifying glimpse into the darker recesses of the Cold War psyche in the USA. No novelist could have invented the relations between David Greenglass and his sister Ethel Rosenberg, nor was the outcome of the case, in which the sister went to the chair largely on the testimony of her brother, free from a vulgar melodrama which Cold War thrillers largely avoided. In Britain the Fuchs case, and those of Alan Nunn May and Bruno Pontecorvo, stirred a different current of public opinion, but one which was quickly submerged in the ongoing obsession with the 'missing diplomats', Guy Burgess and Donald Maclean, who defected to the Russians in 1951, and the 'third man', Kim Philby. This was a story which had an irresistible fascination for students of the British upper classes. Aldo and Shamus registered as 'Burgess' and 'Maclean' at a Parisian hotel in *The Naive and Sentimental Lover*.

In the midst of a fascination with real spies, the reading public warmed to the grandest fantasy-spy of them all, Ian Fleming's James Bond. Fleming's books had at first made little impact upon the reading public. (He jocularly wrote to Somerset Maugham in 1953 that 'My royalties will barely keep Annie [his wife] in asparagus over the Coronation'.) The success of the Bond novels largely dated from the late 1950s, when *From*

*Russia With Love* and *Dr No* became bestsellers. In the England of the Portland spy case (1961), the Vassall affair (1962) and the Keeler–Profumo scandal (1963), James Bond was a culture hero. The ingredients of success in the popular bestseller market in the 1950s reflected something of the material prosperity of the Macmillan era. The fetishism about cars, drink, food and women in the Bond novels was inconceivable in the popular fiction of the inter-war period. The obsessions of the books, which made Bond in le Carré's scathing phrase a 'consumer goods hero' (Crutchley, 1966), raised the objects of consumption to equal billing in the star-system of Fleming's imagination. The villains of the novels were bizarre combinations of physical characteristics which Fleming disliked, or else were modelled upon people he knew. Le Chiffre in *Casino Royale* (1952) was said to be a thinly-veiled portrait of the necromancer Aleister Crowley. Such figures aroused in Fleming a simple response of loathing and, by comparison to Buchan's villains, were possessed of a sexually perverse and insatiable threat. Fleming's villains often have the force of something summoned up from a nightmare, a combination of diverse and intensely personal fears which were brought together in a more simplistic and comprehensible meaning.

What gives Fleming's fictions their power is this sense of menace, this subterranean and aggressive evil, which is invariably subdued and humiliated. Even when the forms of evil become far-fetched, and when in the later books Fleming's creative powers faded and he struggled to sustain his own interest in his increasingly silly plots, they somehow still retain a strange power through their parable-like struggle against evil. This is not the complexity of 'serious' literature, and it is worth recalling how crude a writer Fleming actually was. The fourth chapter of *Casino Royale* begins: 'As two weeks later, James Bond awoke in his room at the Hôtel Splendide, some of this history passed through his mind.' By comparison, the narrative techniques of Childers and Buchan seem quite elegant. Fleming's attitude to women, expressed through Bond, belongs to the same category as Buchan's feelings about foreigners and Jews. Fleming did not take very much interest in the political questions which preoccupied Ambler and Greene, except once in *Casino Royale* where he gives Bond an atypical moment to reflect upon the changing meaning of patriotism:

> Of course . . . patriotism comes along and makes it seem fairly all right, but this country-right-or-wrong is getting a little out-of-date. Today we are fighting Communism. Okay. If I'd been alive fifty years ago, the brand of Conservatism we have today would have been damn near called Communism and we should have been told to go and fight that. History is moving pretty quickly these days and the heroes and villains keep on changing parts. (ch. 20)

Mathis waves away Bond's cautious speculations on the ethics of espionage and murder: 'Surround yourself with human beings, my dear James. They are easier to fight for than principles. . . . But don't let me down and become human yourself. We would lose such a wonderful machine.' This was the moment when Fleming set himself resolutely against the seriousness of Maugham, Ambler and Greene. Action, not ideas or principles, is the common currency of his books.

*

*Call for the Dead* (1961), published by Victor Gollancz in his firm's bright yellow dustjacket, was hardly designed to challenge the dominance of James Bond in the affections of the reading public. Le Carré's first novel was a low-key book, closer to traditional detective stories than to the spy novels of the preceding decade. Le Carré from the first was dealing with the major themes of his later novels, as well as some of the same characters. The plot shows le Carré's fascination with the way reversal can transform the entire meaning of a story. The reversal plots of *The Spy Who Came in From the Cold* and *The Honourable Schoolboy*, in which the actions of Leamas and Jerry Westerby deliberately go against the grain of their assigned missions, are anticipated by the assumption that Samuel Fennan is a spy is overturned by the discovery that it is his wife, Elsa, the German refugee, who is the spy. *Call for the Dead* introduces us to le Carré's most enduring creation, the short, scholarly, patriotic George Smiley, and to Smiley's

41

unfaithful wife, Lady Ann, *née* Sercomb, to his colleague Peter Guillam, a loyal friend in the (unnamed) security service, and to Inspector Mendel, an efficient police inspector given to anti-German outbursts. And with good reason. At one point in the book there is an ambiguous passage of dialogue between Mendel and Smiley which has been famously misinterpreted. Smiley, in hospital after having been assaulted outside a pub, planned to call on Elsa Fennan as soon as he was released.

> Mendel remarked 'She's a Yid, isn't she?'
> Smiley nodded.
> 'My dad was [a] Yid. He never made such a bloody fuss about it.' (*CD*, ch. 11)

This is Mendel speaking, not Smiley. Smiley is, indeed, something of a *luftmensch* who appears in society as though out of the air: he is 'without school, parents, regiments or trade, without wealth or poverty' (*CD*, ch. 1). In the eyes of his wife's social set, Smiley is a puzzle, a man who simply did not fit in. (Shane Hecht in *A Murder of Quality* cruelly reminds Smiley of his anomalous standing, as though it is something shameful.) He is not a Jew, though Jews appear several times in le Carré's books and are generally portrayed with considerable insight and sympathy.

From his first book le Carré places at the centre of the story the intelligence community itself. He portrays the 'Circus', so-named after its location at Cambridge Circus in London, as an institution with a past, a memory, a history. He is the first writer of spy stories to portray the collective historical existence of the security services as an important protagonist. As the story begins, the old days of 'inspired amateurism' live on in memory alone. The Circus is now a large government bureaucracy, much given to intrigue and territorial disputes. The boss is Maston, a civil servant who is the minister's adviser on intelligence. Maston, referred to as 'Marlene Dietrich' by the Special Branch, and as the 'Head Eunuch' by one of the old-timers, is a trial run for the more fully realized Oliver Lacon, who appears in *Tinker, Tailor* in a similar role. Le Carré often allows the service a collective voice, sometimes indistinguishable from office gossip and after-hours shop talk, and it is through such tea-time chat and office reminiscence that the anonymous collective memory of the Circus, and its outstations at Sarratt and Brixton, retrieves its history. Le Carré's use of indirect narration, and the role of speculation and fragments of service history attributed to no one in particular, very effectively gives the Circus an existence which few other writers of spy stories have achieved. Smiley's career, his recruitment while at Oxford in the late 1920s (in the later books, to keep Smiley in motion long after he would have been expected to retire, the date of his entry into the Circus is brought forward to the late 1930s), his work in Germany assessing potential agents, his hatred for the Nazis and his wartime service as an agent for a Swiss arms-manufacturer, all are quickly sketched in, thus planting the crucial seed for the dénouement. This too is an important dimension to le Carré's procedures as a novelist: his characters and his plots are with very few exceptions always rooted in the past – a past which declines to stay buried: it must be dug up, sifted, reinterpreted for clues to the meaning of the present. Sometimes that investigation is a lonely crusade (Harting in *A Small Town in Germany*), in other books it is a collective obsession of the Circus. *Smiley's People* is the supreme example of the quest of a solitary man.

Le Carré's first book begins in the aftermath of an apparent suicide by Samuel Fennan, a civil servant who had been interviewed by Smiley after an anonymous letter was received alleging that he had Communist affiliations. Sent by Maston to interview the dead man's widow, one detail during their talk bothers Smiley: on the evening of his purported suicide, Fennan had placed a call to be woken in the morning. Smiley, too well-trained to ignore the implications of such a detail, finds his doubts about the 'suicide' pushed aside by Maston, who wants a tidy resolution of the case. When a letter arrives the next day from Fennan, urgently requesting an interview, Smiley (not for the last time) feels he can do nothing but resign the service. It is a point of honour. Returning home, he finds a stranger in his house on Bywater Street (a cul-de-sac off the King's Road in

Chelsea), and the plot follows directly from there, along traditional lines. The cars parked in Bywater Street are traced, inevitably one turns out to be hired, and Smiley and Mendel interview the man who rented it. (In his later books le Carré avoids the naïvety of having house-breakers park across the street, in a small cul-de-sac, from their target.) Successive stories are sceptically examined in the best police procedural fashion, until the figure of Dieter Frey begins to emerge. Frey, recruited by Smiley in the 1930s and run as an unusually effective agent during the war, turns up afterwards in the Russian Zone of Germany, and then in London as part of the East German Steel Mission along with Mundt (who was retrieved to play a major role in *The Spy Who Came in From the Cold*). Frey, like Elsa and Samuel Fennan, is a Jew, a man who spoke with the full force of moral outrage (and in this is an early version of Leo Harting) at Nazis and warmongers. He met the Fennans in 1955, and recruited Fennan a year later. The new Germany, rearmed and bellicose, raised nightmarish echoes of the inter-war years. Even after Hungary, it was the dominance of the past, the historical memory of the war and the 'Final Solution' which persuaded Fennan to betray his country.

A piece of tradecraft recalled from the past (and which was employed in *Tinker, Tailor*, when Ricki Tarr's message from Paris summoned Haydon to the safe house) brings Frey out of hiding for a meeting with Elsa at the theatre. Her death, and the Holmesian pursuit of Frey through the night fog, led Smiley to the bridge where he rushes at Frey and pushes him into the dark river to his death. There is no Mathis to pat Smiley on the shoulder and tell him not to worry. He recognizes that Frey allowed himself to be killed. At the crucial moment he chose not to resist Smiley, his old mentor, who feels anything but triumphant at the end of the book.

The final stages of the plot shift to a different and more urgent pace, and the approaching conflict between Frey and Smiley is accompanied by a heightening of the ideological weaponry on Smiley's side, as though it is necessary to transform Frey into a Satanic enemy in order that he might be destroyed:

He [Frey] was the same improbable romantic with the magic of a charlatan; the same unforgettable figure which had struggled over the ruins of Germany, implacable of purpose, satanic in fulfilment, dark and swift like the Gods of the North ... Dieter *was* out of proportion, his cunning, his conceit, his strength and his dream – all were larger than life, undiminished by the moderating influence of experience. He was a man who thought and acted in absolute terms, without patience or compromise. (*CD*, ch. 15)

Judgements of this order are made later in le Carré's career of a far more impressive figure, Karla, but it is interesting to see the terms of analysis already in place in his first book. Frey's extremism, his lack of moderation, marks him out as an enemy. Everything Smiley cares for is the product of an 'intense individualism' and what he particularly hates in Frey is his 'mass-philosophy'. There is an over-inflation about all of this, but Smiley's remorse and puzzlement is ultimately a more mature and sensible reaction than the comic book reassurances which Mathis offers to James Bond.

   It is interesting to note that Frey and the Fennans *care*. They have been touched by the history of their times more profoundly than the others, and have accepted something of its tragic burden. Le Carré does not fail to make us see their selective response to political issues: the occupation of Hungary by Warsaw Pact forces in 1956 did not shake the faith of the Fennans in Communism. Like the security forces, the Communist Party is a small world, a closed community; those doubly within, the spies and moles, possess a heightened conscience, but in an airless environment it cannot grow. (Le Carré made a similar point about the politics of Kim Philby in 1968.) The personal quality which enabled Dieter Frey to live more strongly, and to function so effectively as an agent, carried with it an absence, a deprivation, which is the price he must pay for a heightened life: he is deprived of the moral protection of the middle way. (This is a very *English* point.) Smiley, whose life is dedicated to the cause of moderation, sees what Frey cannot, that enormities like murder and treason committed in the name of high ideals can never be justified. Such means can only taint even high-minded aims.

Smiley feels remorse and puzzlement at Frey's death, but *Call for the Dead* affords little of the vicarious gratifications, the integrative reassertion of the social order, which is such a staple of the spy story within popular literature. The novel ends with a feeling of waste, of depleted energies. The whole Fennan affair is covered up by Maston. The bureaucratic and political needs for a tidy solution leave Smiley, as so often in his career, disgusted with what defending the 'free world' seems to demand. Only the discovery of 'the energy of madness' in himself, the lingering sign that the 'bloodless and inhuman' side of his nature, greatly enhanced by his work in intelligence, had not utterly separated him from the intensity of feeling which Frey and the Fennans know, is a source of consolation.

*

Le Carré's second novel, *A Murder of Quality* (1962), is a deftly written murder mystery comfortably within the conventions of the genre. The wife of a master at an exclusive public school fears that her husband intends to murder her, but before Smiley can investigate – at the request of an old friend from wartime intelligence work – she is found brutally slain. Within the procedures for evaluating motive and evidence there is another story which, in a different culture and age, might have been worthy of Stendhal or Balzac. The attempt of an ex-grammar-school boy to enter the world of Carne School could not be treated with tragic seriousness in post-war England. For that to be possible it would be necessary to believe in the upper classes. Not merely to admire and emulate their manners and style, but to accept that they have an historical mission and meaning which are expressed through their institutions and beliefs, and which are capable of self-fulfilment. *A Murder of Quality* tells, through the conventions of a mystery story, of Stanley Rode and of the 'experiment' which brought him and his wife Stella to Carne. John Braine told the story of a fellow social-climber, Joe Lampton (*Room at the Top* (1957)), basically from within Lampton's subjectivity, and with an ironic bitterness. Such a tone was perhaps unavoidable, given

Braine's subject-matter; but it is notable that le Carré, despite certain aspects of direct personal experience which appear in the book (like Stella, he too was from a Nonconformist family from Poole, and attended public schools feeling very much, in his own estimation, like an outsider) portrays Rode until the end exclusively from the viewpoint of his colleagues, their wives, the pupils at Carne and an outsider like Smiley. The book offered the temptation to subjective feelings, but le Carré declined the invitation.

Carne is one of le Carré's most extreme closed communities. The very battlements of the school seemed to keep the new world out, and the old ways secure. Policemen in Carne may be offered a cup of tea 'in the kitchen' but have no contacts which would reveal the inner world of the school. 'No gossip in the pubs, no contacts, nothing' (*MQ*, ch. 3). The rules of behaviour, the linguistic and social usages, were as though concealed by code:

> You had to be ill, you had to be sick to understand, you had to be there in the sanatorium, not for weeks, but for years, had to be one in the line of white beds, to know the smell of their food and the greed in their eyes. You had to hear it and see it, to be part of it, to know their rules and recognize their transgressions. (ch. 11)

Carne deliberately turned its back to the values of the 'cheaper newspapers'. Stella Rode, in the eyes of the senior tutor, Felix D'Arcy, represented those things, from red-brick council estates to the 'new towns', which Carne scorned. According to the senior tutor, the duty of those at the school was to 'restore and maintain those standards of behaviour which suffered so sadly in the war' (ch. 5).

Fielding, as ever, voices the most sceptical attitude towards the school and its values. He, more than D'Arcy or the other masters, perceives their efforts as having entrenched a ruling class 'which is distinguished by neither talent, culture nor wit; kept alive for one more generation the distinctions of a dead age' (ch. 1). We see him at work, warning his pupils that 'emotionalism is only for the lower classes', and in maintaining the system of values which enables his pupils to scorn the grammar school product, Rode, for his brown boots, and for his wife's 'plebby' manners. Fielding scorns the system, and the 'cult of mediocrity', while sustaining it, and is one of le Carré's most complete portrayals of the paradoxes of class society. D'Arcy, on the other hand, is a believer – in Carne, in the class system, in the gentlemanly code. And it is D'Arcy who in the past supported the attempt to bring people from Rode's background into the school. ' "With careful instruction such people can ... learn our customs and even our manners" ' (ch.5). Years before, he had extended a similarly forgiving hand to Fielding, after the scandal with the RAF lad, and a missionary generosity survives intact. It is only Stella Rode, that 'thoroughly mischievous woman', who declines the opportunity to enter the life of the school.

Ann Snow, wife of one of the masters, thought that Rode was 'terribly Carne-minded'. He had become an Anglican, like the other masters, and had sought to conform socially to the ethos of the community. But the boys notice his brown boots. Smiley is irritated by the way Rode continually struggles to conceal his origins. The famous spy-catcher read the unfortunate schoolmaster like an open book: at the funeral it seems to Smiley that Rode's very walk and bearing 'conveyed something entirely alien to Carne':

> If it is vulgar to wear a pen in the breast pocket of your jacket, to favour Fair Isle pullovers and brown ties, to bob a little and turn your feet out as you walk, then Rode beyond a shadow of doubt was vulgar, for though he did not now commit these sins his manner implied them all. (ch.8)

Rode's origins give him away at once to trained observers (that is the purpose of Carne, to make the boys keen-eyed in the recognition of social difference): the angle of his elbow as he drinks coffee, the way he expertly plucks at the knee of his trouser leg as he sits down, are fatal signs of weakness to Shane Hecht, the 'faded Valkyrie' who preys on any and all signs of human weakness at Carne. Rode's dead wife took great pride in declining to be part of the community. She attended chapel, concerned herself with its charitable activities and took inordinate pride in not welcoming the condescension of her

48

social superiors. Stella was hated, according to Ann Snow, because she did not want to be a lady of quality. She was quite happy to be herself. It is only later, when we are given the chance to see Stella through her husband's eyes, that the woman's pride and bitterness, her manipulative rage, come into view.

*A Murder of Quality* is written with an intensity, and with a grasp of the ways personality is shaped by institutions, which set it apart from the genre of the murder mystery. It is *technically* satisfying as an exercise in detection, but the book has an energy and a seriousness of theme which belies its highly conventional form.

*

Le Carré's third book, *The Spy Who Came in From the Cold*, is an even more considerable technical performance. The plot is the most splendid piece of machinery ever to have been created for a spy story. Leamas is a fake Circus defector to the Abteilung who has been sent to destroy Mundt, the man who rolled up Leamas's agents and who killed Samuel and Elsa Fennan in London. The details of the operation, following Leamas's decline, imprisonment, contact, interrogation and the cross-examination of Leamas during the tribunal, are given with great care. Even more than in his earlier books, details are charged with meaning and become the very life of the plot. The ability to convey them is no mean one. Because details matter so much in his books, le Carré obviously takes great pains to get them right. He takes the same trouble with the location of his stories, travelling widely in the places he writes about, taking photographs, noting down details of scenery, customs, urban landscapes. But James Michener does his homework, and so too does Arthur Hailey. This kind of precision matters, but in itself has more to do with the nature of genre fiction than with imagination and 'literature' as such. The writer's intense concern with detail in turn invites critics to regard factual accuracy as the touchstone of this form of writing. Thus Christopher Hitchins rebukes 'egregious errors of fact and continuity' in *The Little Drummer Girl*, and offers as an example that some-one travelling by land from Beirut to Greece on a *Republic of*

*Cyprus* passport would be inviting unwelcome attention to themselves. The exaltation of fact in genre fiction, and the extension of factoid non-fictional prose, is, however, not so much a way of writing as a substitute for the work of the imagination. But when le Carré cut himself loose from the structure of fact and detail in *The Native and Sentimental Lover*, the common judgement is that he floundered. Le Carré needs the discipline of intricate plots and obsessive detail: that is what his creativity seems to demand. The seriousness of le Carré's concerns and the intricate subtlety of his plot largely deflects criticisms such as that made about the Cyprus passport.

With *The Spy Who Came in From the Cold* le Carré's 'central problem' unfolds. David Monaghan suggests that for le Carré the struggle to remain fully human 'in a society whose institutions have lost . . . connection with individual feeling' (1985, ch. 1) runs through all of the novels. In *The Spy* it might be better to change the terminology a little: the central theme is a conflict between ways of living, and ultimately of social systems, which are rooted in respect for individualism, and those which are not. This theme is argued over, developed and restated with considerable emphasis, and is expressed through a symbol which appears twice in the novel.

Halfway through the book, precisely when Leamas crosses over to East Germany, he recalls a moment in the previous year, while he was hurriedly driving from Cologne to Karlsruhe to meet his agent Riemeck on one of his infrequent trips to the west. While on the autobahn a small car suddenly pulled out in front of him. He flashed his headlights, stamped on the breaks and sounded the horn, just barely avoiding a collision. As he shot past the car he noticed the children in the back seat, 'waving and laughing', and the 'stupid, frightened' face of their father at the wheel. He felt a sudden sense of shock, and pulled off the road:

> He had a vision of the little car caught among them [the giant lorries], pounded and smashed, until there was nothing left, nothing but the frenetic whine of klaxons and the blue lights flashing; and the bodies of the children, torn, like the murdered refugees on the road across the dunes. (*SCC*, ch. 12)

The vision returns as Leamas stands dumbfounded by the dead body of Liz Gold at the end of the book: 'As he fell, Leamas saw a small car smashed between great lorries, and the children waving cheerfully through the window' (ch. 26). And the vision recalls something Leamas saw during the war, when a plane bombed a road clogged with refugees outside Rotterdam. While talking with Control in the second chapter he inwardly thought of the chaos, 'the meaningless hell, as the bombs hit the road'. Both scenes have become symbols to Leamas of the human cost of the great forces at war in our time. The death of the children, which his subconscious conjures up, and the memory of the attack on the refugees are brief passages in the book, but ones which have a significant location (precisely at the beginning, middle and end) and symbolic meaning and resonance which, it will be argued, is an important counterweight to the book's central themes. Le Carré sets symbol and theme in creative tension, and only in the last pages of the book is reconciliation effected.

The book ends with a symbol, not with a fact, a symbol which comes out of a fantasy not uncommonly experienced by parents. Fantasies of physical violence done to loved ones, to children, sometimes reflect feelings which are repressed. Leamas does not imagine that he would be the one to smash the car – that role is assigned to the giant lorries. But in relation to the small car he is a lorry driver. And the fate of the children involved him; he is in some sense responsible for their death. Standing over Liz's body before the Berlin Wall, the connection between the children and Liz is suggested. She has been destroyed, as the children were in the fantasy, and he was responsible. In a sense he has been the author of her death, because he allowed himself the weakness of caring. Had he been stronger and harsher, and not succumbed to the temptation to fall in love with her, Liz would not have been shot by Mundt's men. The political meaning of the symbol is one in which Leamas, too, is implicated. The opposing giant lorry firms conducting the Cold War have taken their toll of innocent bystanders. Liz understood no more of what Control planned and Leamas executed than the children in the small car knew of the reason why the lorries thundered down the autobahn. The symbol conspicuously does not invite us to take sides, to regard one lorry as being in some way better because its driver had virtuous intentions. The effects on others are very much the same. Caught between east and west, Liz was a victim and was dead. No wonder Richard Helms so disliked this book.

On his return from Berlin after the death of Riemeck, Control, with his somewhat 'affected detachment', talks to Leamas about living in the cold. After seeing his networks blown, his agents shot by Mundt, Control wonders whether Leamas can any longer endure 'all this hardness'. '"We have to live without sympathy, don't we?"' (ch. 2). But not without a sense of meaning or purpose: the 'disagreeable' things which we do are done for *defensive* reasons, '"so that ordinary people here and elsewhere can sleep safely in their beds at night"' (ch. 2). Control's schoolboy grin, his belief that '"you can't be less ruthless than the opposition simply because your government's *policy* is benevolent"' (ch. 2), puzzle Leamas, who cannot see what he is getting at. The conversation turns to whether Leamas is interested in taking revenge upon Mundt. This rather puzzling and digressive conversation is one of the strongest justifications, within the politics of the novel, for *our* side. But it is undermined by Control's tone, and the sniggering manner of his speech: he offers in the end a lorry driver's view. The novel does not endorse his words.

Leamas, uncomfortable with Control's donnish and allusive manner, is even less easy with Liz Gold's directness. She persists in asking what he believes in. The answer she receives is calculatedly insulting: '"I believe an eleven bus will take me to Hammersmith. I don't believe it's driven by Father Christmas"' (ch. 4). When she persists, he tells her what he doesn't like (Americans and public schools) but evades the question. Later that evening Liz tells him that she believes in 'History', which brings forth a laughing realization that she was a Communist. Le Carré's handling of Leamas's beliefs is problematic. He is an officer, an agent, not an ideologist, and is assumed to perform his work without elaborate philosophical or political justification. Control's simplistic explanation of the difference between us and them seems to Leamas unnecessary.

After three days of interrogation in Holland with Peters,

Leamas is flown east where he is handed over to Jens Fiedler, Mundt's deputy in the Abteilung. Fiedler, too, asks about the 'philosophy' of those who worked in the Circus, and of Leamas himself. Leamas cannot give an answer, so he replies to Fiedler as he had to Liz Gold: "'I just think the whole lot of you are bastards'" (ch. 13). But Fiedler is a patient man, with much to gain from a thorough knowledge of Leamas's mind. He offers an argument for the Abteilung, a felicific calculus of the fight of socialism for 'Peace and Progress': "'so many women, so many children [killed]; and so far along the road'" (ch. 13). The hypothetical act of terrorism, which Fiedler blandly accepts, was a bomb placed in a restaurant. The image of the victims of the struggle for 'Peace and Progress' is connected with Leamas's fantasy of the small car and the waving children. Fiedler willingly accepts the burden of carnage, while Leamas is sickened and deeply disturbed. Fiedler points out that a Christian society, for which life is sacred, may not draw up any such balance sheet between progress and death, ends and means. But Leamas, following Control, says that even Christian societies have to protect themselves, in effect that they cannot be less ruthless than their enemies because their values were higher.

The dialogue between Leamas and Fiedler establishes the idea of the congruence between the east and the west. Their values may be utterly different, but the logic behind their defence is identical: in Fiedler's words, '"The exploitation of individuals can only be justified by the collective need"' (ch. 12), and, in the next chapter, '"a movement which protects itself against counter-revolution can hardly stop at the exploitation – or the elimination, Leamas – of a few individuals"'. Fiedler points out that the Circus, no less than the Abteilung, has engaged in such 'exploitation'. There is a 'growing identity of interest' between the two. Later in the book Fiedler's belief is further strengthened: '"We're all the same, you know, that's the joke"', he says to Leamas (ch. 18). It is only at the end of the scene, when Leamas momentarily pulls himself psychologically from the role he has been playing as 'Leamas the defector', that the immediate and tactical significance of this interplay becomes clear. Leamas is content to allow Fiedler to believe that the two services share a similar logic: it eases his path into Control's plan, and ultimately is responsible for his downfall. The congruence of east and west, which exists through symbol, is here allowed merely a tactical significance. The tension between the theme, established in Leamas's conversations with Liz, Control and Fiedler, and the symbol of the children in the car, gives *The Spy Who Came in From the Cold* some of its uneasy energy.

Le Carré is often very careful to undercut the professed beliefs of his characters. The demolition job he does on Liz Gold is excessively effective, and in the end leaves her an object of pity. The paperback classics in her apartment are unread; the Communist Party she belongs to, and which le Carré describes with scathing brilliance, was a cosily deceiving 'little world'. When she attends a branch meeting in Leipzig it reminds her of party meetings in Bayswater, and when she used to attend mid-week evensong in church (why would a nice Jewish girl have been going to church?), 'the same dutiful, little group of lost faces, the same fussy self-consciousness, the same feeling of a great idea in the hands of little people' (*SCC*, ch. 19). And Liz Gold, the library assistant, is very much one of the 'little people'. After her appearance before the tribunal Liz is taken to prison, where she has a contrived talk with the vigilant socialist wardress. Liz asks about the purpose of the prison, and is told that it is for 'traitors', 'brain workers', intellectuals and other reactionaries and enemies of the people who 'defend the individual against the state'. When she learns that Fiedler and Leamas were to be shot, she is stunned. If only Leamas had trusted her, had told her what he had to do:

> surely he knew her well enough to realize that in the end she would do whatever he said, that she would take on his form and being, his will, life, his image, his pain, if she could; that she prayed for nothing more than the chance to do so? (ch. 24)

She now realizes the full horror of the tribunal, for whether she lied or had told the truth, or stayed silent, she has been responsible for destroying a fellow human being. As a child she had been horrified to learn that with each step she took minute creatures were killed. Communism to Liz was an expression of her idealistic and tender-hearted nature, but she has been caught up in a situation in which she can only cause pain to others. It is at least some consolation that the nice Fiedler and Leamas are on the same side. When Mundt takes her to join Leamas, Liz at first cannot understand why they are being freed. The truth, that Mundt was London's man and that the operation had been aimed from the start at Fiedler, takes a moment to sink in. Leamas tells her that, in the service, she has been nothing more than an 'operational convenience'. Her role would have been equally as effective whether she and Leamas fell in love or not. She has been 'exploited' with ruthless effectiveness.

Leamas admits to feeling ashamed and angry at what has been done, but he cannot judge the matter with the simplicity of others, for there is a large risk in the operation. ' "London won – that's the point. It was a foul, foul operation. But it's paid off, and that's the only rule" ' (ch. 25). He attacks and ridicules her scruples, for her beloved Communist Party was no less ruthless. Leamas says that the death of an innocent man can be justified on 'party terms', exactly as Fiedler had done: ' "A small price for a big return. One sacrificed for many" ' (ch. 25). It was war, but nothing to compare with the last one for wastage. The point has no effect on Liz, for whom the human reality of the operation has a terrible meaning: Leamas's service, and Mundt's, sought to ' "find the humanity in people, in me and whoever else they use, to turn it like a weapon in their hands, and use it to hurt and kill" ' (ch. 25). (Jerry Westerby, thinking of Lizzie Worth, comes to a similar conclusion and fate in *The Honourable Schoolboy*.) They were the same, in the end. When they get out of the car at the Wall Liz walks stiffly, numbly; she is already in effect dead, a victim of the Cold War. And so too is Leamas, who cannot, after what has been done, see any reason to save his life by jumping down on the west side of the Wall. Liz, so vulnerable a character, presents the concluding meaning of the novel. Control's assurance that there is a fundamental difference between them and us cannot survive her experience. She has been used cynically in the name of higher ideals which stink in the nostrils. Le Carré does not show the Circus to be notably more concerned for the individual than the East Germans are. Fiedler was right: they are the same. The issue, as he presents it here, is not so much between ways of life which defend individualism and those which do not, as between the human factor, the sympathetic impulse and the perception of people as 'operational conveniences'. Smiley found the operation 'distasteful' and wanted no part of it. Control did not agree with his feelings. In the end Leamas shares the same moral ground as Liz: "'but everywhere's the same, people cheated and misled, whole lives thrown away, people shot and in prison, whole groups and classes of men written off for nothing'" (ch. 25). Along with its intricacy and detail, the real literary merit of the novel has a great deal to do with anger, disgust and the nausea Leamas felt as he walked the streets after he saw Riemeck killed.

It is an angry book, written by a man who has the instincts of a moral radicalism that is seldom seen in English literature today. For a moment at the beginning of the book the bright searchlights of the East German border police catch Riemeck 'like a rabbit'. The same lights, suddenly switched on, catch Liz and Leamas with their 'savage accuracy' (ch. 25), before they too were shot. It is Leamas who, rushing down the autobahn to meet Riemeck, turned his headlights full on to warn off the small car with the children who waved in the back seat.

# 2

## CLOSED COMMUNITIES

John le Carré's fourth book, *The Looking-Glass War*, appeared in the early summer of 1965, but it conveys little sense of the moment of its publication. *A Small Town in Germany*, published three years later, is filled with references to the events of the late 1960s. The earlier book represents a different strategy for le Carré, a calculated placing of the novel in a closed, airless environment insulated from the turbulent events which followed upon the first Labour administration in two decades and the deepening slide of President Johnson and the American people into the war in Vietnam. The subject of *The Looking-Glass War* is the intelligence community itself, wrapped in nostalgic dreams of wartime glory, and only touched tangentially by the life of the larger society. In *A Small Town in Germany* le Carré's subject is the self-absorbed diplomatic world of the British Embassy in Bonn and its subtle capacity to resist the challenges posed by an idealist from within and a threateningly reborn demagoguery in the streets. Together, le Carré's novels of the second half of the decade explore the nature of closed communities and their ability to persist in the face of challenge and social change; they offer a powerful and pessimistic image – not only of the bureaucratized world of diplomats and security services but also of the paralysis of the British official class itself.

*

At the end of *The Looking-Glass War*, when the farmhouse near Lübeck is being scoured of any trace of their presence, and when Haldane, Leclerc and Johnson were preparing to return to England and abandon their agent, Leiser, John Avery begged for them at least to listen to Leiser's last transmission. They had created Leiser, pumped him full of faith in the Department, sent him on a dangerous mission into East Germany and were now leaving him to certain death. Avery bitterly pointed out that Leiser was 'Peter Pan's last victim'. They had all conspired to play Peter Pan, romantically imagining that England had an independent role still to play on the world stage. Avery, the youngest of the Department team which sent Leiser on his 'run', is the only one who cares about their betrayal. Haldane tells George Smiley, who has come to warn them that the mission has been blown, to thank Control for the rope which they have used to hang themselves. Leclerc deftly turns to other concerns, while Avery buries his face in his hands and sobs. The others ignore him as they tidy up the farmhouse. The novel ends with a particularly desolate sense that the security services in general, and this particularly forlorn version of an RAF intelligence department, consist of people who live in an emotional and moral vacuum and who deceive each other, as they deceive those they recruit and train, into beliefs which sustain the unreality of their own lives.

*The Looking-Glass War* is a sustained examination of the inner decay of British intelligence. The structures survive, but the belief in their purpose, the sense of charismatic mission, have decayed. Le Carré writes with incomparable authority on the particular smell of national decline, the unforgettable dusty, rusting, padlocked streets of south London, and the bureaucratic grubbiness of the Department: '"We're dead, don't you see?"' Haldane reminds Leclerc. Rarely has the equivalence between secret service and the health of the society as a whole been so aggressively asserted. In his introduction to the study of Philby by Page, Leitch and Knightley (1968), le Carré describes the security services as a place in which, once entered, no further personal or spiritual growth would be possible. Insulated from the 'cleaner air of the outside world', those, like Philby, who were on the inside would have been left with assumptions and values untouched. (But where, in all of le Carré's fiction, is that 'cleaner air' to be found?) *The Looking-Glass War* is a study of a closed community, and of the costs paid by those who belong to it, the price, in other words, of playing Peter Pan.

Senior figures within the department share recollections of the war. There are wartime photos on the walls of Leclerc's office. ' "It was simpler in those days" [he recalls]. "We could say they'd died for their country" '. But when he tries to console Taylor's widow with the idea that her husband had died a 'gallant' death, she rebukes him: ' "What do you mean, gallantly? . . . We're not fighting a war. That's finished, all that fancy talk" '. Patterns of work established during the war, when officers spent the morning debriefing air crews, determine the Department's current expectation that junior staff would arrive by half past nine, while the senior staff (who, in truth, scarcely know how to fill their day) arrive by mid-morning. The Alias Club, reminiscent of the quiet club in Manchester Square which Steed-Asprey founded and of which Smiley was a member (*CD*, ch. 11), has wartime photos on its walls, and is a haven for wartime friends whose 'tired and watchful eyes have no horizon to observe'. Avery is sent on his 'run' with a passport for a man named Malherbe: the name was selected because Leclerc had had a relationship with Malherbe during the war. Leiser is trained on wartime techniques, in Oxford where the Department ran its wartime operational training programmes. To retrain Leiser they seek out Johnson, their wartime expert on wireless telegraphy, but thanks to clever bureaucratic manœuvring on the part of the Circus, they have to make do with a transmitter of wartime vintage. Leiser himself is an agent they ran during the war, now settled down to civilian life in London. For everyone except Avery, who was too young, the comparison of 'those days' and the present is unavoidable and demoralizing. Adrian Haldane, more cynical and cautious than his colleague Leclerc and who, like Fielding in *A Murder of Quality*, remains within a system in which he no longer fully believes, sees how things have changed: ' "It's a different game now. In those days we were top of the tree – rubber boats on a moonless night; a captured enemy plane; wireless and all that" ' (*LGW*, ch. 5). Even for the cynic Haldane memories of the war survive in romantic sepia tones. (In *Call for the Dead* Dieter Frey was destroyed because he continued to use a favourite piece of tradecraft from the war.)

The reality of life in the Department, and in England, is grey, threatening extinction to everything they ever believed in. The Circus, which swallowed up the Department's Polish desk in 1948, seemed anxious to absorb their fabled registry as well, but did not intend to help them reactivate agent networks. Haldane insists that '"They want us to go to sleep, not go to war"'. The Department has declined in size since the war, and can no longer afford to run its own couriers. Avery must be sent to fetch the roll of film which Taylor was bringing back to London. The decline in their fortunes is reflected in the present location of the Department in a 'crabbed, sooty villa' on Blackfriars Road. They all remember the glory days during the war, when they worked out of a building on Baker Street.

In the face of so many signs of decline and decay, the desiccated inner life of the Department persists in its old forms and beliefs. Taylor, who seemed to young Avery 'a dreary English bore, straight off Brighton pier', affirmed the basic continuity of purpose of the Department. The job was the same, and they were fighting for the same values and goals. Taylor's external style is of a man who had served in a 'decent' regiment, and belonged to 'decent' clubs. But when Leclerc visits Taylor's flat, he is shocked by the dinginess of the neighbourhood. Even more interesting is Leclerc's feeling of shame. 'This was not the society they protected, these slums with their Babel's Tower: they had no place in Leclerc's scheme of things' (*LGW*, ch. 3). That a member of his staff should live in such a place seemed to offend the very notion of Englishness that Leclerc carried within himself. 'Englishness' for such a man as Leclerc is a romantic and heroic concept; he remains loyal to a vision of a life which had once given the nation heroic meaning. The war years were the time when personal identity fused with national purpose. The Department, even in its diminished size and exile in south London, embodies for men like Leclerc that heroic moment.

Personal relations within the Department, and within Department marriages, tell quite a different story. Avery senses Leclerc's vulnerability. It is something he shares: he, too, is an inadequate, unhappy person who wants to believe, to feel consecrated by a sense of national purpose. Haldane reserves his most savage rebukes for Avery, suspecting that the young man's yearning was a criticism of his own lack of belief in anything other than technique. Avery's wife Sarah, who was unwell, asks *why* was it so important for him to go to Finland when she had a fever and couldn't cope? His flaccid generalizations fail to convince her (or the book's readers) that his work mattered 'terribly', for herself or for anyone else. Sarah Avery, a desperately unhappy woman, does not share her husband's yearning to believe, his adolescent desire to be patted on the back and told that he had served the nation well. His gratitude is directed to Leclerc, who gave him responsibilities and a faith to believe in. But in the confusion of his own feelings, in loneliness, he seeks contact with others: he wants to touch Carol, his secretary, but they both 'gently' recoil from physical proximity with nothing said. He is also disturbed by the intensity of Leclerc's emotions, and his assertive physical presence. For a 'sickening moment' Avery wonders whether Leclerc is going to put his hand on his knee. The relationship with his wife is dead and corrosive; that with Carol is unspoken and unconsummated; with Leclerc Avery veers between hero worship and sexual fear. It is only with Leiser that Avery constructs a relationship, finds a purpose in despair. (Le Carré returns to the subject of failed marriages, and the attempt to find purpose outside the constraints of marriage, in *The Naive and Sentimental Lover* (1971): it is a theme which he has often placed in the near-background of his central male figures like Stanley Rode, Smiley, Avery, Karla, Becker, Magnus Pym and lesser figures such as Lacon and Peter Worthington.)

Le Carré makes perhaps overly abundant use of religious metaphor to describe the Department, and the men who work in it. They are all 'doubting clerics', 'black friars', who huddle together hoping to keep their personal faiths alight. They live in an 'arid land', in a 'wilderness of abandoned faith', denouncing each other for lack of belief, or for believing too easily. Avery's wife penetratingly describes him as someone who has loyalty without faith. Leclerc attacks Haldane's pessimism and his lack of belief in the transcendent purposes of the service. And because he has no faith, Haldane cannot understand why Leiser accepts the mission: '"I mistrust reasons. I mistrust words like loyalty. And above all I mistrust motive"' (*LGW*, ch. 11). Leclerc and Haldane regularly use the idea of a 'second vow', an act of faith made in the direct confrontation of doubt, to describe the commitment the Department ultimately requires. Haldane makes his second vow when he agrees to head the special section which will train and run Leiser, though he lacks faith in the mission and contemptuously doubts Leiser. Leclerc uses the idea of the second vow to explain risks which are taken, missions planned and executed, precisely to resolve doubt. When Leiser expressed doubts about wireless transmissions sent on the same basis as they had done in wartime, Johnson reassures him: you've taken the vow, don't worry. (The phrase appears in James Kennaway's diary entry from March 1965 as a way to describe the 'yellow letter' he wrote to his wife Susan after their estrangement (*The Kennaway Papers*, p. 103).)

In Adrian Haldane's opinion, Fred Leiser is 'a singularly unpleasant person' who – like Smiley – dresses like a bookie. His suitcase is 'a little too orange for nature', and his coat is not a true 'British warm'. He does not realize the extent to which he speaks in clichés, and even Johnson corrects his usage. (Le Carré has an extraordinarily acute feeling for the subtle gradations of English snobbery.) Having served as an agent with the Department during the war, Leiser is retrieved by Haldane for the operation into East Germany with a clever combination of flattery and lies. The 'old crowd' are still running the show, the 'war rules' are in force and, Leiser is told, the Department is as big and as busy as ever: little lies, leading to a big lie: that they remember Leiser, had kept his file to hand and still regarded him as one of themselves. Haldane briefs Avery on the way to handle people like Leiser: maintain Leiser's illusions that the Department remains exactly as it was. '"And remember, he's British: British to the core."' (Affirmations of national self-identity run throughout the whole of le Carré's work, as talisman and reassurance.) The operation against the East Germans wasn't half as clever as that which the Department organizes against Leiser. What they sell to the credulous Leiser is what they wanted to believe about themselves: that the Department was competent, successful and a worthy repository of Leiser's trust. Leiser declines to demand guarantees about the running of his business when on the mission ('"I'm working for English gentlemen"'), a detail nicely counterpointed with the meeting at the ministry with the under-secretary, at which Leclerc's request for a pension for Taylor's widow is frostily rejected. These 'English gentlemen' are liars, cynical manipulators and know nothing of integrity.

The relationship between Leiser and Avery, who superintends the training course at Oxford, is like that which unaccountably grows between Leamas and Liz Gold in *The Spy Who Came in From the Cold*. At first it is a matter of casual physical contact, an open hand laid on Avery's back, an arm on his shoulder. Avery feels uneasy at this unEnglish behaviour, but then comes to accept it with laughing amusement and contentment. Theirs is the warmest relationship in the novel. Walking down the street Leiser slips his arm through Avery's who, in reply, presses Leiser's hand captive beneath his arm 'and they continued their walk in shared contentment, forgetting the rain or playing with it, treading in the deepest parts and not caring about their clothes' (ch. 12). Practising unarmed combat, the two men are brought into fierce embrace, only to be softened with a smile. The exploration of their growing intimacy is one of the great strengths of *The Looking-Glass War*. Avery's wife Sarah, without knowing what was developing between the two men, senses the change in her husband. He seems to her like someone who was in love. '"You looked free and at peace"', she remarks, as though that constituted a further indictment in the ongoing hostilities of their marriage. Leamas desperately sought to keep Liz Gold out of the operation against the Abteilung, but Avery was specifically responsible for maintaining Leiser's morale; his job is to keep him happy. In doing so he nourishes Leiser's illusions while earning his affection. It was that act of love which, for Haldane, constituted Leiser's second vow. Avery persuaded Leiser to *like* his controller, but rages against the reality of what he has done:

'You made me do it for you, made me love him! It wasn't in you any more! I brought him to you, I kept him in your house, made him dance to the music of your bloody war! I piped for him, but there's no breath in me now.' (ch. 22)

And there's none in Leiser. He tells the German girl Anna a little story before the Vopos arrive to arrest him. One day, while walking by the river in London, he came upon an artist drawing with chalks on the pavement. It was raining, and the picture washed away as it was being created. The subject of the picture, 'dogs, cottages and that', hints at a register of experience remote from the Department and the lives of those who work for it. The pavement artist and his picture is an elusive symbol for the myth-making of Leclerc, Haldane and Avery. In the end they can walk away from the whole thing. Like good bureaucrats they survive to function another day. The immediate task is to disown Leiser and blacken his reputation. Leiser, who believed that he is working for English gentlemen, and remembering Avery's 'warmth and English decency', faced the Vopos with an erect posture, 'conscious of tradition' to the end. Talking to Philip Oakes in 1977, le Carré expressed some of the bitterness which *A Looking-Glass War* so powerfully expresses:

> I really loathe the games they [spies] play. . . . The game justifies their very existence. They're all fantasists talking endlessly about team spirit, which I take to be a euphemism for homosexuality and reiterating the myths they create around themselves as monotonously as banging a ball against a wall.

Leo Harting, Leiser's direct counterpart in *A Small Town in Germany* (1968), is also a foreigner, a man who believes in the values which the British embodied, who is destroyed by the fatal disproportion between things as they are and as they might be. The novel, set in the British Embassy in Bonn where le Carré was posted, is an intensely realized picture of a closed community. The world of *The Looking-Glass War* looks back to the past: all of the characters function in the shadow of the Second World War. There is a much stronger sense of the political tensions of the mid- and late 1960s in *A Small Town in Germany*. The overriding concern of the British diplomats in the novel is the fate of negotiations which were taking place in Brussels over British entry into the EEC. (In fact, while le Carré was writing the novel the French President de Gaulle blocked the attempt by the Wilson government to open negotiations. The desperateness of the British political situation, as portrayed in the book, gives the negotiations a poetic if not historical rightness.) The Rhodesian embargo is mentioned. The British Army on the Rhine has been 'added to our strategic reserve in the United Kingdom'. There are anti-Vietnam demonstrations in England and race riots in the USA. Posters demanding an end to 'Coca Cola culture' appear in Bonn. Student demonstrations have taken a violent turn; a British library has been sacked. And there is a populist-nationalist politician in Germany, Karfeld, who raises many nightmares of the recent Nazi past and who wants to open talks with Moscow about reunification. (Tony Barley, 1986, suggests that Karfeld and his movement bear a strong resemblance to von Thadden's NPD, a mass movement of the radical right which achieved some electoral successes in mid-decade.) It is not yet 1968, but many of the ingredients are coming into place. All of this happens off-stage in the novel, as a background to the *mentalité* of the community of British diplomats.

A minor official within the embassy has gone missing, and with him are a number of politically sensitive files. The Foreign Office sends out Alan Turner to deal with the issue but, in view of the difficult situation in Germany, he is told to 'go lightly' and not stir up unnecessary trouble. (Smiley is summoned with similar instructions to tidy matters up at the beginning of *Smiley's People*.) The novel portrays his interviews with the staff of the embassy, and his growing understanding of the missing man, a German national named Harting who has worked for the British since the end of the war. The simplicity of the story, in which the central figure, Harting, remains absent throughout, resembles Ambler's *The Mask of Dimitrios*; like that novel, we see Harting through his relationships with his colleagues. Le Carré's concerns, however, root the story in the relationships between the ambassador (de

Lisle), the head of chancery (Bradfield), the chancery registrar (Meadowes), the information officer (Jenny Pargiter) and the investigator from London, Alan Turner. *A Small Town in Germany* is a thriller of ideas – about beliefs, national decline, class consciousness and Englishness.

The senior figures within the embassy, de Lisle and Bradfield, are favoured individuals, members of the club. De Lisle, 'an elegant, willowy, almost beautiful person', was the popular incarnation of the 'brilliant English diplomat'. Bradfield, responsible for the political section of the embassy, was a cool, correct, efficient diplomat, blessed with a beautiful wife, Hazel; though Catholics they are pillars of the embassy staff's religious observance. Together they maintain the surface appearance of the diplomatic mission, but as Turner explores their knowledge of Harting another sort of picture emerges: of men bitter at the decline of Britain, and who regard its retreat as something akin to personal betrayal. (Haydon, the traitor, came from the same social ethos, and had similar feelings about the fate of the country.) The picture they paint of Britain's place in the world was, in the late 1960s, the common change of public discussion. Their reflections might have been transcribed from the editorials and letter pages of *The Times* and the *Daily Telegraph*: '"Our credit is exhausted, our resources are nil"', Bradfield admits. '"We may be bankrupt, we may beg for loans, currency and trade; we may occasionally . . . reinterpret . . . our Nato commitments"' (*STG*, ch. 4). Turner senses the bitterness Bradfield feels, the 'family shame', at the withdrawal of the Army from Germany, and the scrapping of three-quarters of the Navy. '"It was our worst time; our most humiliating time"' (ch. 4). De Lisle and Bradfield belong to the class which was raised with the sense of imperial mission and national importance. The shrunken Britain of the 1960s offends their self-image. De Lisle expresses, perhaps more completely than any other character in le Carré's novels, the nihilism and despair which such men felt at the national decline. Their anti-Americanism continually reappears: America the strong, America the hopeful, offends them as much on grounds of taste and style as for political reasons (*vide* Haydon). De Lisle tells Turner that '"I see no hope at all for the future, and it gives me a *great* sense of freedom"' (ch. 4). The Americans rampage through the present, not understanding why the British are so much 'nicer' to each other, sharing as they do a condemned cell. De Lisle does not believe in democracy: only a government by alienation is left; and the governmental 'policy' which diplomats were supposed to implement leaves him with confusion: '"*I* don't know what I'm defending. Or what I'm representing; who does?"' (ch. 7).

It is Bradfield who articulates the most coherent response to the decay of purpose, and who elevates hypocrisy into a uniquely English form of salvation. He utterly refuses Turner's suggestion that they openly inform the German Minister of the Interior, Ludwig Siebkron, that Harting was a spy and had absconded with embassy files. '"I will not have it *said*!"' The Germans could think what they liked about the missing man. Bradfield insists that the facade be maintained, despite well-informed German suspicions. Later he delivers an important lecture to Turner about appearances. Harting has broken the surface, disturbed the outward calm of the embassy. '"I am a hypocrite . . . I'm a great believer in hypocrisy. It's the nearest we ever get to virtue. It's a statement of what we ought to be"' (ch. 17). Bradfield serves the appearance of things. He has enlisted in the task of serving a weak and corrupt nation, but would far rather fail as a power than 'survive by impotence': better English than Swiss. He expects nothing: '"I expect no more from institutions than I expect from people"' (ch. 17). Along with de Lisle he articulates the despair of his class.

Alan Turner is as 'common as a mongrel' and has a pronounced Yorkshire accent. He is referred to as 'The Bevin Boy'. Brought from an obscure family background and St Anthony's College, Oxford, to the Foreign Office, he is still an angry man, someone who cares. Shawn says of him: '"You'd pull down the whole forest . . . to find an acorn"' (ch. 3). His interviews with Bradfield and de Lisle, and with the rest of the embassy staff, reveal how little his urgency is shared. Bradfield belittles the idea that Harting is an important figure, or that his disappearance meant anything of significance. Harting is a 'child' in politics, a 'complete innocent'. He renewed Harting's contract (like Fielding in *A Murder of Quality*, the insecurity of

Harting's position has an important influence upon his relations with the embassy staff) more out of pity than any other reason, especially when Harting seemed exceptionally anxious to take on the personalities survey. Gaunt, a Welshman in the chancery, is too trusting to check on Harting's activities, and he positively resents Turner's aggressive suspiciousness. Meadows also is disinclined to 'go sniffing round asking who's looking at what', but like Bradfield he notices the change which takes place in Harting, and his obsessive work in the chancery files. Jenny Pargiter loaned the duty officer's keys to Harting: '"I had to trust him. It was an act of giving. Don't you see? An act of giving, an act of love"' (ch. 8).

It adds up in Turner's eyes to a classic case of a long-term penetration agent, a mole (though the word 'mole' does not appear in le Carré's books until *Tinker, Tailor, Soldier, Spy* in 1974; Michael Straight, 1983, recalls that the term was in use in left-wing circles in Cambridge in the 1930s). The ethos of the Foreign Office disarms them before such men: the friendships, the mutual trust, the instinctive faith in personal relations above institutional security, is damned by Turner. He senses something else in the accounts he receives of Harting. The snobbery he observes within the embassy seems to represent the fundamental character of the 'Club': that Harting had no background, no education, no breeding; that he was worth a drink but not dinner (Bradfield: 'He wasn't quite dinner party material' (ch. 4)); that he was 'Unpromotable, unpostable, unpensionable', explains a comprehensive system of class-consciousness. The truth of Harting's relationships, especially that with Bradfield, surfaces later, and as it does Turner's understanding of Harting alters dramatically. But already Turner, the spycatcher, and Harting, are seen to '"form a team of your own. You're the other side of the wire. Both of you"' (ch. 7). The observant Siebkron subtly mentions to Turner that it has been noticed that he and Harting had '"*many* things in common"' (ch. 10) and he receives a beating from Siebkron's men. Turner and Harting are fundamentally outsiders, disliked for their persistence which verges on the fanatical. They both want to penetrate beyond the corrupt maintenance of appearances, and to proclaim their truths. They were both, in their own ways, believers in the absolute virtue of the truth. But, as Bradfield reminds Turner, '"There are no absolutes here"' (ch. 16). Bonn and its mists constitute a morally neutral ground, where all values lose colouration: de Lisle and Bradfield are the men in power in the Bonn Embassy, while Harting, with his personal mission, his 'absolutes', dissembles on the margins, and is in the end flushed out and destroyed by men more ruthless than himself. Harting is betrayed by his old comrade Praschko and disowned by the embassy. Turner alone wants to save him from Siebkron, to do honour to his ideals – an idea which Bradfield finds incomprehensible. The British taught Harting certain notions of truth and 'absolute justice' during the war. Nuremburg and the attempt at denazification was another promise. Turner argues with the stony Bradfield that they made Harting what he was, made him see things. But in the world in which only appearances matter, there was no effort Bradfield could conceivably make. Turner suggests that it was a personal matter, that Harting had been disowned because he was the lover of Hazel Bradfield. Harting's offence, Bradfield tells him, was against '"the built-in moderation of an aimless society"' (ch. 17). The 'romantic clap-trap' of protest and conscience, the dream of freedom and transcendence, are ultimately in pursuit of something which doesn't exist. Harting should have forgotten what happened during the war. He has broken the 'law of moderation', and has been destroyed. (Virtually identical terminology is used in *The Quest for Karla*.) Turner passionately affirms his own belief in the romantic dreams of freedom and justice, but Bradfield has wedded himself to forgetting, to the task of learning how not to look and how not to feel. During the conversation, which occurs in the last chapter in the novel, Bradfield turns from the river to face Turner, with small tears in his eyes. With that touch Bradfield becomes no less tragic a victim of the age than Harting.

*

*The Naive and Sentimental Lover* had a disastrous critical reception in 1971 ('the narrative limps along' (*Listener*), 'The book is a disastrous failure' (*The Times Literary Supplement*), 'the product of self-indulgence and intellectual laziness' (*Spectator*)). It was not without admirers: Graham Lord described it in the *Sunday Express* as 'the most interesting novel I have read this year'. It would be nice to say that the critics had got it wrong, and that this novel, the author's only attempt to break away from 'spy stuff', was a better and more interesting book than the reviewers allowed in 1971. It is certainly a book which seems now more interestingly of its age, of the Britain of the 1960s, than was understood.

It is written in short, discontinuous passages, sometimes as little as a snatch of dialogue or a brief description of mood or place. It is odd how those who criticize le Carré for the heaviness of his prose could overlook the quickness of this novel's movement, its sense of the fluidity of character and portrayal of the shifting nature of relationships. This form of discontinuous narration serves to shake our confidence in the events portrayed, and as scenes loop back over themselves an ontological uncertainty is thrown over the whole novel. Did Shamus and Helen ever exist? What actually happened in Paris? It contains passages of an experimental nature unlike anything in le Carré's prose:

> Elise and Mrs Bluebridge floated hand in hand, intoning sweet phrases from Old Hugo's good book; respectful waiters clapped to him in rhythmic unison; sinners and strivers, toiling up God's hill, turned to watch him with approval. The chorus multiplied. Oui, *Burgess*, oui. *Ça te fait plaisir? Beaucoup de plaisir, Elise.* In Kensal Rise the green lights switched excitedly while the band played a Sherborne song: *Vivat rex Edwardus Sextus! Vivat!* The girls looked on, no longer dancing, studying respectfully the master's effortless technique. No mothers with prams appeared among the crowd, waving, thanking, owing him their babies. (*NSL*, ch. 27)

Le Carré has brought together here many levels of the experience and memory of Aldo Cassidy, from the prostitute which he and Aldo picked up in Paris (who *may* have been nothing more than a sexual fantasy) to his experience as a schoolboy and his pram-manufacturing company; it captures his sexual fantasy of masterful technique, at a time of deeply unrewarding congresses with his cool wife Sandra, and anticipates the impregnation of his secretary Angie. There are strong passages of sexual and dream fantasy in *The Naive and Sentimental Lover* and a narrative technique which deliberately seeks to make complex an experience which, in truth, is the staple of hundreds of humdrum novels. The discrepancy between the simplicity of the story of a stale middle-aged businessman's desire for romantic excitement, and the complexity of the narrative medium, lies at the heart of the artistic problems of the novel. (In *The Quest for Karla* a similar tension between simplicity of story and fanatical complexity of narrative is present: in that larger work the ultimate signification is made more complex by its historical dimension.)

There is in the extravagance of Shamus, the struggling, affectionate, drunken novelist, a problem of a different order. Shamus quotes Dylan Thomas, and was compared by reviewers to Brendan Behan. He embodies Bohemianism, the artistic impulse struggling against the bourgeois world. But since his artistic talent is solely a matter of hearsay, and since neither his wife Helen nor Aldo seem to have read his only published novel, Shamus is simply tedious, brutal, drunken and violent. Le Carré has ducked the problem of portraying a real artist, and of confronting the situation which artists actually face in post-war England. He is far more sucessful in imagining a terrorist or a minor diplomat than a man engaged in his own line of work. The affection Shamus engenders in Aldo is frankly incredible although, as the relationship between Avery and Leiser suggests, and that hinted at between Bill Haydon and Jim Prideaux, the relationship between men in his books is every bit as much a minefield as that between men and women. There is a little too much hinting and teasing here, too many kisses launched jokily between the two men and then left unconsummated, to feel that the meaning of such relationships for le Carré has been fully explored.

What is wrong with *The Naive and Sentimental Lover* is not that it isn't a spy story, but that it ultimately lacks the subtle historical dimension which gives his other books their extra level of meaning. The sense in which the embassy in Bonn

71

stands for the state, and ultimately for the society which it represents, is absent in this novel. The commercial interest represented in Aldo Cassidy's pram-manufacturing company is the kind of thing which someone who had never worked in business, who had never manufactured anything, might conjure up. The hints of Japanese competition, on the far horizon, serve to illuminate a dimension of the novel which, however peripheral to the main plot, suggests why this book lacks the historical sense. The company makes parts used in the manufacture of prams: it is a traditional firm, started by Aldo's father in a garage, and is now successful and prosperous. Aldo is far more concerned with personal problems than those posed by the business, and at the end retires to the countryside to lead the life of a mildly adulterous businessman turned country gentleman. It is as though le Carré took his leading character out of Martin J. Weiner's *English Culture and the Decline of the Industrial Spirit 1850–1980* (1981). A decade later Aldo's firm would probably have been declared bankrupt, prams having generally been supplanted by lightweight push-chairs imported from the Far East. Substance for at least angry thoughts about national decline, failure of nerve, suicide of a nation: themes which appear elsewhere in le Carré's books but are absent here. He cannot envisage the fate of a manufacturer as of the same historical meaningfulness as that of a servant of the state: a modest example, perhaps, of Weiner's theme.

It is hard to know how much of the story of *The Naive and Sentimental Lover* is autobiographical. The relationship between 'David' and James and Susan Kennaway, the trip to Paris, the episode in Switzerland, including the madness of Shamus and 'the hating, violent person' who arrived at the train station when 'David'/Aldo and Susan/Helen were about to depart, all appear in *The Kennaway Papers*. It is clear that it doesn't ultimately matter how much or how little of the novel is autobiographical: its success and failure as a novel is our only proper concern here. If it had been written by someone else, by David Cornwell perhaps, it might have been seen to be an interesting and by no means wholly unsuccessful example of an experimental novel. From John le Carré, however, it was 'a disastrous failure'. His readers were, by and large, unwilling to accept this kind of book from him. The tyranny of popular taste is not to be ignored, but it is a pity that some other conclusions were not drawn from *The Naive and Sentimental Lover* than those which sent le Carré, tail between his legs, back to the Circus.

# 3

## THE REASONABLE MAN AT WAR

In an essay published in 1939, E. M. Forster wrote: 'I hate causes, and if I had to choose between betraying my country and betraying my friend, I hope I should have the guts to betray my country'. The portrayal of Bill Haydon in *Tinker, Tailor, Soldier, Spy* (1974) translates the ideological treason of Philby into a story about the betrayal of personal relations. Le Carré *Forsterizes* the Philby story. Despite the presence of the great political issues of national decline and the Cold War it is the human betrayal, and the human price paid for that betrayal, which give the book its central focus.

Haydon appears in the novel as a romantic figure, admired by his colleagues as a living reminder of the heroic days of British imperial greatness. No one spoke of Kim Philby in such terms. His father, St John Philby, was an arabophile, a noted author, explorer, sometime friend and colleague of T. E. Lawrence, the advisor to King Ibn Saud of Saudia Arabia, one of those Englishmen who delighted in the wearing of Arab dress. ('I feel guilty', Lawrence wrote to D. G. Hogarth in 1927, 'always in his [Philby's] eyes: guilty of being an unscientific traveller' (Garnett, 1938).) Le Carré has transferred some of the romantic associations of Philby *père* to Haydon, 'our latter-day Lawrence of Arabia'. Kim Philby was sent to Westminster School, where he was a King's Scholar, and remained, in the eyes of his friends, a 'very public school' type. (Toby Esterhase, in his 'lofty, artificial Englishness', sends his son to Westminster, as did le Carré.) Philby with his slight stammer and mouse-brown hair was rather ordinary looking. At Trinity College, Cambridge, from Michaelmas 1930, he joined the university Socialist society and switched over to read economics after doing the part I history tripos. He was abstemious, rather poorer than many of his contemporaries at Trinity, and was probably destined to become one of those balding former civil servants who are a touch too proud of their collection of Left Book Club titles. By comparison with the flamboyant and socially prominent Guy Burgess and the brilliant Donald Maclean, Philby passed through Cambridge without being much noticed. The general election which brought the National Government to power took place soon after he returned to Cambridge for his second year. The collapse of the Labour Government, and the effective end of an electoral route to social reform (given the size of the National Government's majority), began a process of political disenchantment and re-examination which ended in 1933 with a lifelong commitment to Communism. The glamorous Oxford of Haydon, who was at Christ Church, seems closer to Guy Burgess's experiences at King's, as does the implied relationship with Jim Prideaux. Burgess had been an Oppidan at Eton and was a notorious seducer of young men. If Philby was methodical and private, Burgess was curly-haired, handsome, boyish, entertaining, sexually voracious, neurotic and self-indulgent.

The representative figure of Cambridge Communism in the mid-1930s was John Cornford, a blazingly dedicated, intense and romantic Marxist. Burgess, on the other hand, was persuasive, decadent and something of an intellectual *flâneur* of the left. At Cambridge he was a member of the Pitt Club, noted mainly for the drunken carousing of its members, and he was an Apostle, the secret society which prided itself on recruiting the most brilliant men of their generation. Michael Straight, who was a fellow-Apostle (and who was recruited into the Communist Party by Anthony Blunt), gives a vivid picture of Burgess in his autobiography, *After Long Silence* (1983):

on a closer look, you noticed the details: the black-rimmed fingernails; the stained forefinger in which he gripped his perpetual cigarette stub; the dark, uneven teeth; the slouch; the open fly. (p. 94)

Haydon's office, with its aura of 'undergraduate mayhem, monkish and chaotic', the 'customary dottiness' of his dress, the spectacles jammed up into his hair, his art of fostering affection and the filthy state of the mews cottage he shared with his girl in Kentish Town ('there was a smell of oil paint and baby'), suggest Burgess, not Philby, as the model. In fact, Haydon is a careful amalgam of both men: he is a complete spy, as devious and effective as Philby, and as vivid and fascinating as Burgess.

Le Carré was in the Intelligence Corps in Austria when Burgess and Maclean defected in 1951, and was at the British Embassy in Bonn when Philby disappeared from Beirut in January 1963. *The Spy Who Came in From the Cold* appeared while interest in the 'third man' was still intense and was on the bestseller lists when Guy Burgess died in Moscow in September 1963. Within weeks of the ending of the BBC television production of *Tinker, Tailor* in November 1979, Anthony Blunt was unmasked as the 'fourth man', giving an extraordinary timeliness to le Carré's novel. The story of Philby, Burgess, Maclean and Blunt has for three decades been an obsession of the British, long out-lasting public interest in the cases of Alan Nunn May, the Krogers or George Blake. More recent spy cases seem now to pass through the media without leaving much of a residue in public memory. (Who, in fact, was Michael Bettaney?)

The Philby case held a mirror before the British ruling class, and the betrayal it reveals is more important by far than the treason of a Lord Haw-Haw during the Second World War and similar cases: for what Philby and his friends did was to betray 'the Set', as George Smiley's wife, Lady Ann, might describe them, the close-knit ruling and administrative class of Britain. The Rosenbergs in the USA, with their proletarian, scientific and Jewish backgrounds, would probably not have ever been in a position to become important spies in Britain. (Their fate, it is worth remembering, was not shared by any of the British spies, who when caught were given long prison sentences and then were quietly exchanged with the Russians.) Burgess and Maclean fled during the Festival of Britain year, that carefully choreographed assertion of national pride and economic recovery. Philby fled several months before the Profumo scandal broke. The Blunt revelations were one of Mrs Thatcher's first crises after coming to office in 1979. The case would not be forgotten, and raised its head, with sometimes devastating effects, at moments of crisis and uncertainty. Philby is the bad conscience of the establishment, the betrayal which shook their self-confidence and the automatic assumption that people like themselves *were* the nation.

\*

At the centre of *Tinker, Tailor, Soldier, Spy* is a political debate which took place in a Delhi prison in 1955. The scene has the stumbling slowness of a dream: only one person speaks throughout (Smiley), but the significance of what is said, and not said, takes us to the heart of the novel, and of the larger struggle between Smiley and Karla which is played out across the three novels of the *Quest*. This is the only moment in nearly a thousand pages of fiction when the two protagonists meet, until Karla crosses over into West Berlin at the end of *Smiley's People*. It is perhaps a pity that he did not attempt to do with Karla what he so successfully does with Smiley, to give the doctrine, the 'fanaticism', a living place within a fully realized character. Karla is nothing more than his fanaticism. The consequence of this one-dimensional characterization is that serious political debate is simply not present in a book in which it should be. He is not, of course, the writer to restage Koestler's *Darkness at Noon*, with its extended debates on revolutionary morality. I don't think he is really interested in political ideas, at least not in the fashion of Koestler for whom the human (let us say the Forsterian) dimension was weaker than the ideological contention. Karla, and what we might infer he stands for, which can hardly in the real world be reduced to 'fanaticism', is a significant absence in these novels.

Le Carré presents the scene in the gaol, as recalled by Smiley during a quiet, reflective after-dinner discussion with Peter Guillam. Karla had been picked up by the Indian police after a tip-off was received that he was heading to the USSR from the USA, and Smiley, knowing him only as a fairly minor Moscow Centre agent named Gerstmann, went out to offer the usual package for low-grade defectors of asylum in the west in return for co-operation. Even in the post-Stalin era a sudden recall to Moscow could mean execution or a sentence in the work camps, but Karla sits silently through Smiley's rehearsal of the commonsense arguments for self-preservation. The man's 'watchfull stillness' disturbs Smiley, who is sweating profusely and feeling uneasy before Karla's calm. In desperation he begins to talk of Karla's 'Ann', and to suggest that they might be able to do something to help her. Going back would inevitably make things worse. (The full horror of Karla's marriage plays an important role in the third volume of the *Quest*.) Smiley, whose own marriage had come near collapse, was himself not sure whether he would be returning to unfaithful Lady Ann. A similar 'embarrassed kinship' disturbs Smiley when he interviews Peter Worthington in *The Honourable Schoolboy*. (Male bonding – in the relations between Leamas and Fiedler, Avery and Leiser, Turner and Harting, Aldo Cassidy and Shamus, as well as Pym and Axel in *A Perfect Spy* – has been a continuing and intense concern in le Carré's novels.) The more he talks the more Karla's silence draws him deep into his own confusions. Returning the next day, with only a couple of hours before Karla's plane was due to leave for Moscow, he again presents the commonsense reasons for defecting to 'Gerstmann'. But he sees in Karla what he hopes to find, a reflection of his own values, and a hint in the Russian's face that he is, like Smiley, superior to mere dogma. Had they not, through their different routes, come to something of the same conclusions: 'That in the hands of politicians grand designs achieved nothing but new forms of the old misery?' (*TTSS*, ch. 23). The notion that individual life meant more than 'the sense of duty, or obligation, or commitment' (ch. 23) was a very Forsterian, liberal and western way of expressing a philosophy of life. Jokingly Smiley describes himself to Guillam as, at that moment, the 'very archetype of a flabby Western liberal' (ch. 23). Karla sat silently, but takes the cigarette lighter which Smiley's wife had given to him. It is somehow 'expressive of the bond between us' (ch. 23). And he returns to Moscow, without saying a word in return.

In this remarkable scene Smiley voices the logic of a political position, or perhaps of a political temperament, which is set in direct opposition to that of Karla. While Smiley pleads and perspires, revealing himself to be the complete creature of the liberal individualism of his culture, Karla is his negation. Neither considerations of personal safety nor the well-being of others sway his resolve to remain coolly silent. He is 'fireproof' in Guillam's eyes, someone who couldn't be bought or black-mailed, who 'would rather die at the hands of his friends than live at the hands of his enemies' (*SP*, ch. 12). While trying to persuade Karla to defect, Smiley tried to imagine himself in Karla's position and to use this as a weapon against the other man's silence. Later in the book, Smiley suggests that the same device was used by the mole 'Gerald' to draw Percy Alleline into the handling of 'Merlin': the idea that the Russian spy was a spokesman for a dissident group appealed to Alleline, and gave him something to identify with. He saw himself in a similar situation. Smiley tried to exchange his own position with that of Karla, in what was at one level a clever approach to interrogation. It is also a gesture expressive of Smiley's nature, his conscious recognition of the humanity even of those who were his enemy. He allows himself to believe that Karla is 'accessible to ordinary human arguments'. Although that assumption is mistaken in 1955, it remained as the fundamental basis for Smiley's approach to espionage, the 'temple of his private faith'. He does not agree with Guillam that Karla was untouchable: '"Karla is not fireproof because he's a fanatic. And one day, if I have anything to do with it, that lack of moderation will be his downfall"' (*SP*, ch. 22). 'Moderation', 'compassion', 'humanity' and its cognate formulations ('his concept of a reasonable balance in human affairs' and 'We're fighting for the survival of Reasonable Man' (*HS*, chs 5, 15)), on one side, fanaticism, absolutism and inhumanity on the other: thus the structure of values in *The Quest for Karla*.

The larger structure of the *Quest* portrays the dissolution of such firm certainties. Karla the absolutist is undone by 'excessive love' and 'compassion' while Smiley, the reasonable man, pursues and destroys his foe with unbridled 'fanaticism'. The presiding metaphor is of frontiers breached, values drained, ideologies confused and confounded. 'We have crossed each other's frontiers, we are the no-men of this no-man's-land' (*SP*, ch. 27). The structure of that dissolution is remarkably complex. Raymond Chandler once granted to a correspondent that he didn't formally plan the complex plots of his novels: he began them, and if they were right they grew, if not he started over again. (This showed in the books rather more than Chandler imagined.) Le Carré's books cannot possibly have been written without elaborate planning. What is so remarkable about them is the simplicity of the 'story' and the extraordinary elaboration of the 'plots'. *The Quest for Karla* may be boiled down to three stories: how a Russian mole within British intelligence is unmasked; how the attempt of a Russian mole in China to escape is uncovered by the British and the Americans; and how Karla, attempting to provide for his daughter in a Swiss sanatorium, is detected and then forced to defect. The stories as they are plotted often have a simplicity of larger shape combined with a remarkable complexity of plot. While reading le Carré we pass from the complex to the simple. Consider the longest of the three novels, *The Honourable Schoolboy*. Analysis of the plot might suggest a classic structure of *exposition* (the discovery of the gold seam), *initiating action* (the departure of Jerry Westerby for Hong Kong), *rising action leading to the crisis* (Jerry's approach to Lizzie Worth, the pressure on Drake Ko, the trip to Cambodia to see Ric, ending with his disappearance from the American base in Thailand when ordered to return to London), *falling action* (the death of 'Sarratt man' in Jerry, the rescue of Lizzie and the attempt to warn Drake Ko), and the *dénouement* (the seizure of Nelson Ko, the death of Westerby, the replacement of Smiley at the Circus by Saul Enderby).

It is Smiley, the moral centre of gravity of le Carré's imagination, who humanizes this vast machinery of plot. Since Smiley so peremptorily wound up Leclerc's ruinous operation in East Germany in *The Looking-Glass War*, nearly a decade passed before he reappeared in *Tinker, Tailor*. In the intervening period le Carré has to some extent rethought Smiley, abandoning several important themes from the earlier books, while retaining others. The tendency of Smiley's work to enhance the bloodless and cerebral side of his character, so acutely diagnosed by Elsa Fennan in *Call for the Dead*, and the suggestion recalled by Smiley from a wartime description of himself, that he possessed 'the cunning of Satan and the conscience of a virgin' (*MQ*, ch. 9), were too crude to sustain. The 'energy of madness' which causes the death of Dieter Frey equally seems to have faded. What remains in the *Quest* of the Smiley of the earlier books is his podgy and ill-dressed figure (' "Looks like a frog, dresses like a bookie" ', according to Inspector Rigby), his passionate belief in individualism and an 'earnest formality'. It is part of the legacy of the spy story that the act of reading the people he comes into contact with is a central and instinctive dimension of his work. It is in the variety and subtlety of his 'reading' of Elsa Fennan, Dieter Frey, Fielding and others that Smiley shows the skills which will be so central to the *Quest* trilogy:

> Smiley was fascinated by Fielding, by his size, his voice, the wanton inconstancy of his temperament, by his whole big-screen style; he found himself attracted and repelled by this succession of contradictory poses; he wondered whether he was supposed to take part in the performance, but Fielding seemed so dazzled by the footlights that he was indifferent to the audience behind them. The more Smiley watched, the more elusive seemed the character he was trying to comprehend: changeful but sterile, daring but fugitive; colourful, unbounded, ingenuous, yet deceitful and perverse. (*MQ*, ch. 5)

In his meetings with Elsa Fennan and Stanley Rode we see another side of Smiley, his capacity for sympathy. His voice seemed to offer Fennan 'strength, comfort, compassion and safety'. Smiley's response to Rode is more complex, showing as he does the pathos of the schoolmaster's attempt to gain a place in the world of Carne School. He felt 'a movement of sudden compassion' as a parent might feel for a child who remained 'hopelessly apart, hopelessly alone'. There is inevitably a double meaning in Smiley's sympathy and compassion. His attempt to project himself into Karla's situation in the Delhi gaol was more than sympathy, and so too is his response to

Fennan and Rode: there is a need to manipulate, to control, which finds compassion as effective an instrument as any other. Several times in *The Looking-Glass War* Smiley speaks out quite sharply against the tendency in espionage to put too much trust in technique. Haldane, in particular, is scathingly described as someone who made technique a way of life 'like a whore . . . technique replacing love'. But even towards such blusterers and cynics as Leclerc and Haldane, there 'was nothing in Smiley's face but compassion, nothing in his voice but that dreadful patience with which we speak to the insane'.

Compassion in Smiley is wedded to scepticism, and to the conviction that 'there isn't any truth about human beings, no formula that meets each one of us'. After his painful pursuit of Haydon, Smiley shrugs off the difficulties of fathoming the man's nature. He is distrustful of the 'standard shapes' of human motive, and 'settled instead for a picture of one of those wooden Russian dolls that open up, revealing one person inside the other, and another inside him' (*TTSS*, ch. 39). The Circus ethos makes them all uneasy before the question of motive. Analysts like di Salis, leg-men like Prideaux and Westerby, as well as senior officers like Haldane (in *The Looking-Glass War*) dismiss attempts to pin down either their own motives or those of their colleagues. It is far easier simply to accept communal values without endless self-scrutiny. But le Carré presents such figures, whether idealists like Harting, deceived innocents like Leiser, or the limited but essentially virtuous men like Westerby as all in a sense self-deceived. In their world ideology and belief, the whole terrain of motive, become a question of personality. There are those who believe in nothing, the perfect men for the fogs of Bonn. ' "There are no absolutes here" ', Bradfield tells Turner. ' "It is all doubt. All mist. The mist drains away the colours. There are no distinctions" ' (*LGW*, ch. 16). For Roy Bland values were merely a 'spiel' which he once accepted. The only thing which has any meaning in England now, he tells Smiley, is self-interest: ' "It's the name of the game these days: you scratch my conscience, I'll drive your Jag, right?" ' (*TTSS*, ch. 17). Lacon rather fumblingly admits that he too cannot see any *purpose* in what they are doing: ' "Difficult to know what one's aims are, that's the trouble, especially if you're British"' (*TTSS*, ch. 10), and his wife melodramatically confides to Smiley that '"Oliver thinks we're *doomed*"'. Haydon's woman Jan angrily demands to know '"who the bloody hell believes in government any more"' (*TTSS*, ch. 38). The characters in le Carré's books express the bleakest scepticism before all values, all forms of understanding; and those who are not sceptical are 'naive', and pay severely for their trust. (The decay of 'Sarratt man' in Jerry Westerby is subtly done.) Smiley is one of the chief vehicles for doubt in the books in which he appears, and it is doubt, scepticism and vigilance which makes him a brilliant intelligence officer. But he is also the custodian for certain positive values, not the devotion and gratitude which he points out to Westerby, nor any Cold War ideology of anti-Communism, but precisely the compassion with which he goes about his work. 'Compassion' is not an alternative to the moral ambiguities of the work Smiley does, it is not a way to save himself, or his service, but it is, at least, the irreducible nub of humanity. It is the degradation of compassion, the relegation of it from end to means, which enables him to defeat Karla, and which gives us a sense that no one has clean hands in that world, neither the Galahads like Westerby nor the embodiment of western liberalism.

The Smiley of the *Quest* conducts a sequence of interviews which are important devices for plotting. They give the successive novels a kind of rhythm, a pattern, which persists within the complex and diverse unfolding of the plot. They also serve to establish at greater depth the inner circle of Circus personnel. In *Tinker, Tailor* Smiley travels to Oxford to visit Connie Sachs, and then seeks out Esterhase, Bland, Haydon, Sam Collins, Max (who was with Jim Prideaux in Czechoslovakia), Jerry Westerby and then Prideaux, before doubling back. The interviews are marvellously well written, with an understated economy of effect and characterization which makes each a revealing vignette. Smiley is probing their memories, and also perhaps their loyalties: Bland and Esterhase are no less suspects than Haydon. And when some of the same terrain is retraced in *The Honourable Schoolboy* and *Smiley's People*, we see one of the structuring devices of the trilogy. Connie's new life running a kennel with Hilary ('a proper pair of raving whatsits' (*SP*, ch. 15)), and the changes in Lacon, the breakdown of his marriage, the contemptible way he has adjusted to each shift in political atmosphere in Whitehall, are neatly registered. So, too, the change in Esterhase into the 'Mr Benati', the art dealer on the wrong end of Bond Street. The interviews in *Tinker, Tailor* are obsessively concerned with the events of one night, when news came that 'Operation Testify' had been disastrously betrayed, but in *The Honourable Schoolboy* Smiley conducts the interviews with Lizzie Worth's abandoned husband, with her parents, the Pellings, and with the missionary couple who had known Drake and Nelson Ko as children in China. In each interview Smiley conceals his true identity, and with delicacy allows the pathetic schoolmaster who married Lizzie, her *Telegraph*-reading parents and the gentle missionaries to reveal themselves.

Each interview shows Smiley playing a different role. With Jerry Westerby, for example, he exudes a firm confidence, a clarity of purpose, which has sometimes been misunderstood. He assures Westerby that

> A lot of people see doubt as a legitimate philosophical posture. They think of themselves in the middle, whereas . . . really they're nowhere. No battle was ever won by spectators, was it? We understand that in this service. We're lucky. Our war began in nineteen-seventeen, with the Bolshevik Revolution. It hasn't changed yet. (*HS*, ch. 5)

Westerby *needs* oversimplification, the little cowboys-and-Indians games; Smiley knows that 'the only way to talk to Jerry was to talk like Jerry's newspapers: short sentences; facile opinions'. (The interview with Westerby in *The Honourable Schoolboy* has a parallel with the meeting between Leamas and Control in *The Spy Who Came in From the Cold* (ch. 2) in which Control probed whether Leamas was suffering from 'metal fatigue'.) Smiley asks Westerby if he was '*prepared*', and had the will-power for a difficult mission. The Cold War flavour of Smiley's speech to Westerby directly contradicts earlier expressions of his attitude towards anti-Communism, such as that in *Tinker, Tailor* in which it was stated that 'Smiley had always been a little embarrassed by protestations of anti-Communism' (ch. 17). This too was the ethos at Sarratt, where there was little patience for 'the fiery-eyed zealot who grinds his teeth and says, "I hate Communism"' (*HS*, ch. 18). It is necessary to say one thing to Westerby, while feeling rather differently within himself. The difference between these two passages does not reflect a political shift on Smiley's part, but is part of the moral ambiguity demanded by his profession.

This is not to say that there are not changes in Smiley: the structure of the *Quest* is based upon such an assumption. But it is change rooted in Smiley's moral sense, and not in directly expressed political opinions. It is how one might expect Forster to portray such a transformation. The difference may be seen in Smiley's reaction to Leamas's mission in *The Spy Who Came in From the Cold*, which Control describes: 'He finds it distasteful. He sees the necessity but wants no part in it. . . . He is like the surgeon who has grown tired of blood. He is content that others should operate' (*SCC*, ch. 6). When Leamas thinks of Smiley's actions after his departure to East Germany, especially the attention to Liz Gold, it seems almost a conscious attempt to wreck the operation: 'He must have had a crisis of conscience, thought it was wrong to kill or something' (*SCC*, ch. 23). Smiley is a man of conscience in a service more comfortable with technical than ethical questions. He had more than once resigned from the Circus on matters of principle. But when news reached London that Frost had been tortured and killed for revealing details of Karla's account at a Hong Kong bank to Jerry Westerby, Smiley merely remarked: '"The response was more than we expected. Operationally nothing is amiss. Operationally we have advanced the case"' (*HS*, ch. 14). Later he weighs up the gains from the operation for Westerby's benefit:

> 'Billions of dollars and thousands of men could not obtain a part of what we stand to gain from this one operation. A war general would laugh himself silly at the thought of such a tiny sacrifice for such an enormous dividend.' (ch. 20)

There is a debate in *The Spy Who Came in From the Cold* about ends and means which helps to put into perspective this theme in *The Quest for Karla*. Fiedler accepts the logic behind the view that the 'collective need' justifies the 'exploitation' of individuals. The Abteilung man's confidence that this view is shared by the Circus is at first part of the delusional snare into which he was drawn, but in the end it proves all too true. London won, and if Leamas is 'exploited' and Liz Gold made an 'operational convenience', the means justify the end: 'Intelligence work has one moral law – it is justified by results' (ch. 2). This is the logic which Leamas accepts when he returns home in disgrace from Berlin, and it is the same assumption which guides Fiedler's judgement on the defection of Leamas: '"The operation was successful. Whether you were worth it is questionable. We shall see. But it was a good operation. It satisfied the only requirement of our profession: it worked"' (ch. 12). The ground had been well prepared before the publication of the *Quest* for the convergence of values and the erosion of frontiers. Smiley accepts the logic of the service; however, he tries to temper it with compassion and humanity.

One of the ways this convergence is portrayed is through observations on the part of Saul Enderby and Connie Sachs that he and Karla were '"Twin cities . . . you and Karla, two halves of the same apple"' (*SP*, ch. 15). Another is the way the 'price', the means to the end, is assessed. After Prideaux was captured in Czechoslovakia he was exchanged for the Czech networks which the Circus had established. Max reminds Smiley of the details:

He started counting. 'Pribyl', he began, touching his thumb. 'Bukova Mirek, from Pribyl's wife the brother', he took a finger. 'Also Pribyl's wife', a second finger. A third: 'Kolin Jiri. Also his sister, mainly dead. This was network Aggravate.' He changed hands. 'After network Aggravate come network Plato. Come lawyer Rapotin, come Colonel Landkron, the typists Eva Krieglova and Hanka Bilova. Also mainly dead. That's damn big price, George' – holding the clean fingers close to Smiley's face – 'that's damn big price for one Englishman with bullet-hole.' (*TTSS*, ch. 27)

(A large part of the force of this passage resides in the brilliant capturing of the emigré's English, and the use of gesture.) Smiley hopes to use Haydon to save 'in humanitarian if not professional terms' what remains of the Czech networks (*TTSS*, ch. 32). He desperately tries to locate any survivors, and arranges with the Cousins for an 'exfiltration' through the Crimean port of Sochi. In the event the escape fails, the agents are shot and Martello calls personally to console Smiley: '"Can't go down the line for every one of them. That's generalship. So you just remember that"' (*HS*, ch. 3). Smiley once spoke in his usual oversimplified vein to Westerby about his gratitude towards the service, and the chances it has given him to 'pay' for all it has done for him. Jerry, in his own fashion, agrees: '"We *made* Bill"', ran his argument, '"so it's right we should carry the brunt of his betrayal. Pay, in fact. Pay. What old George was on about"' (*HS*, ch. 18). After he escapes from Fawn and Guillam, Westerby recalls Smiley's words, only they had now taken on another meaning. His mind is on Frost, the bank official he 'burned' for the Circus, who is now dead, and on his friend the journalist Luke, also killed by Drake Ko's men. '"Trouble is, sport," he thought, silently addressing Smiley, "the paying is actually done by the other poor sods. Like Lizzie, for instance"' (*HS*, ch. 20). Lacon with unwitting irony returns to this theme when he drunkenly describes the things which hold together people like himself and Smiley: '"We're birds of a feather, George. Both patriots, givers, not takers. Trained to our services. Our country. We must pay the price"' (*SP*, ch. 20).

Max and Westerby point out the changes that have taken place within Smiley in the pursuit of his 'black Grail'. Neither are complex or subtle men, and their very 'simplicity' gives a particular authority to their moral sense. They have not been corrupted by the 'moral law' of espionage, that ends justify means. To the extent that Smiley has been corrupted, he speaks in paradoxes:

> To be *inhuman in defence of our humanity*, he had said, *harsh in defence of compassion*. To be *single-minded in defence of our disparity*. (*HS*, ch. 19)

Peter Guillam recalls these words from a chat Smiley had with senior officers, who angrily resent his habit of taking his faith out and polishing it until the flaws showed. But the context is governed by the psychotic violence of Smiley's factotum, Fawn, who was only too willing to hurt, and without such quasi-philosophic scruples: 'Fawn was lurking, hoping for another excuse to hit him'. The context changes the meaning of Smiley's words. The inhumanity (of Smiley's use of Karla's daughter) comes close to rivalling Karla's plan to have Haydon become Lady Ann's lover; the harshness he refers to has more than metaphoric meaning for Westerby; the single-mindedness of Smiley's quest verges on obsession. Guillam quietly congratulates Smiley after Karla has been taken away: '"George, you won"' (*SP*, ch. 27). In his modest and off-hand manner, Smiley says '"Did I? . . . Yes. Yes, well I suppose I did"'. The final irony is that the Reasonable Man has lost far more, in human terms, than he has won. But then for spies there are no 'human terms', and Smiley shows us why.

*The Quest for Karla* is a work on the scale of similar projects in post-war fiction by Paul Scott, Lawrence Durrell, Doris Lessing, Anthony Powell and C. P. Snow: substantial trilogies, quartets and even longer sequences have been so pronounced a feature of the contemporary British imagination that le Carré's place within this tradition is worth asserting. *The Quest* contains exactly the vast range of characters and scenes, the subtlety of social observation, the responsiveness to national character and national decline, the tortured unease of the relations between men and women, and the symbol-making power, which such ambitious sequences have embodied. Le Carré's choice of title suggests, however, that a 'meaning' for the events described has been provided, and it is this decision which separates his books from the most interesting examples of the tradition I am relating them to. The choice of title lets the trilogy down by allowing a narrower sense to attach to the whole, and perhaps something of an *ex post facto* interpretation; the title denies the trilogy full seriousness.

# 4

## FAMILIES

Buried deep in le Carré's imagination, and at the heart of his troubled humanism, there lies a horror of manipulation, a belief that the calculated use of feelings for 'professional' reasons constitutes a violation of personal integrity, trust and the basis for the 'human bond'. Yet manipulation is part of the necessary arsenal of espionage. (Novelists are, in their work, the most extravagant manipulators of all.) Manipulation and betrayal are central to the general structure of corruption and falsehood in the world of his novels. Whether for high ideals or cynical ones, for the 'free world' or in the name of collectivist tyranny, the result is much the same: people are viewed instrumentally, as means instead of as ends. Liz Gold rages at Leamas for what his people had done: '"to find the humanity in people . . . to turn it like a weapon . . . , and use it to hurt and kill"' (*SCC*, ch. 25). Leo Harting in *A Small Town in Germany* deliberately seeks to win the confidence of the embassy staff while pursuing his own private demons. When Turner interrogates Gaunt, Meadowes and Jenny Pargiter they each proudly admit their trust of the missing Harting. Trust is the proud badge of their humanity. '"I can't go sniffing round asking who's looking at what, can I?"' answers Gaunt; for Pargiter trusting Leo Harting is an act of love. (It is by no means clear that they were wrong to do so.) In *Tinker, Tailor* Karla coldbloodedly intends to obscure Smiley's professional judgement by putting Bill Haydon in Lady Ann's bed. After Haydon's death, Smiley thinks of the victims, Prideaux, Max, Sam Collins, Connie Sachs, Jerry Westerby and of the others whose 'personal loyalties' were broken by Haydon: 'Nothing is worth the destruction of another human being. Somewhere the path of pain and betrayal must end'. But in turn Smiley no less ruthlessly uses Karla's feelings about his daughter Tatiana to trap and destroy the Russian (*Smiley's People*). Part of what detaches Jerry Westerby from his Sarratt training is the dawning realization in *The Honourable Schoolboy* that the man he is so mercilessly pressing, Drake Ko, is rather like his own father, and acted merely out of family feelings to bring his brother out of China.

Le Carré's two most recent novels, *The Little Drummer Girl* (1983) and *A Perfect Spy* (1986), portray the family, the nourishing community, as the central stage upon which spy and terrorist, counter-spy and counter-terrorist, function. Since *The Naive and Sentimental Lover* he has not dealt with the inner dynamics of family life. He uses the family rather as an abstraction, the promised land of caring and virtue, from which his characters are exiled. The family is an idea, a compact, a hope; the real relations between men and women in his work are often painful, frustrated and destructive.

The whole topic of le Carré's women is an intriguing one. From his earliest work it is clear that le Carré's is a masculine world, and that the relations between men constitute the central terrain of his portrayal of the human situation. From the margins, so to speak, he has created a succession of complex, 'difficult', sometimes unattractive women who provide a crucial and largely hostile perspective upon his male characters. Some are shrewish destroyers (Shane Hecht, Stella Rode, Grigorieva), bedraggled victims (Sarah Avery, Stella Craven), or a mixture of the two (Elsa Fennan); others have been innocent or willing dupes (Jenny Pargiter, Hazel Bradfield). Maria Ostrakova is a sole essay in peasant sturdiness; in Tatiana he has created a pure, mad victim. They all have roles to play and are vividly drawn, but they are not agents in their own right, and do not in themselves sustain the weight of meaning which is rooted in relationships between men in le Carré's books. (This is made explicit in *The Looking-Glass War*, where the relations between Avery and Leiser and his relations with his wife Sarah are specifically contrasted.)

Le Carré's techniques of characterization of his female

figures have grown in strength and subtlety over time. Compare his Elsa Fennan:

> It was a worn face, racked and ravaged long ago, the face of a child grown old on starving and exhaustion, the eternal refugee face, the prison-camp face. (*CD*, ch. 3)

and the Gothic and melodramatic description of Shane Hecht:

> Shane was so hideous. Massive and enveloping, like a faded Valkyrie. All that black hair. (*MQ*, ch. 1)

with Doris Hibbert:

> A daughter sat with them, thirty to forty-odd, blond, and she wore a yellow frock and powder but no lipstick. Since girlhood, nothing seemed to have happened to her face beyond a steady fading of its hopes. When she spoke, she blushed, but she rarely spoke. She had made pastries, and sandwiches as thin as handkerchiefs, and seed-cake on a doily; to strain the tea she used a piece of muslin with beads to weight it stitched around the border. (*HS*, ch. 11)

Although Hibbert is a character who plays virtually no role in the plot, and would have been eliminated by a writer more determinedly interested in keeping the story humming along, le Carré's characterization of women has passed from their being essentially embodiments of ideas to the more poetic practice of constructing character through scene and symbol. The temptation to *tell* rather than the Jamesian decorum of *showing* is still evident, but the overall effect is more complex. (There is, occasionally, a disfiguring snobbery in le Carré which is more often directed towards women than men, as in his description of the audience for the 'Heretics' tour of Devon and Cornwall: 'Their audience was the headscarf-and-lentils brigade, whose drugged, envious eyes told you they would do better than you if they ever sank so low as to try' (*HS*, ch. 17), and the ghastly dinner party which Aldo and Sandra attend at the home of the Eldermans in *The Naive and Sentimental Lover*.)

With Lady Ann, who seldom appears directly, and Lizzie Worth in *The Honourable Schoolboy*, a new attention is present. Lady Ann cuckolds Smiley, and the significance of that act reverberates throughout the trilogy. It is a betrayal more insidious and threatening because she does it for love, for an ideal of self-fulfilment which blows apart the polite fictions governing married life. That she has been cynically manipulated by Haydon in the process adds yet another layer of irony. She is observed and puzzled over: 'He loved her, he was indifferent to her, he observed her with the curse of detachment' (*SP*, ch. 20). It is a characteristic moment for le Carré's men, who seem sincerely puzzled by the ontological status of women: 'Jerry wondered what it must be like to inhabit such a beautiful body, living up to it twenty-four hours a day' (*HS*, ch. 13). Aldo Cassidy in *The Naive and Sentimental Lover* stands deeply puzzled by Sandra and Helen: '*I don't know how you're made: that's the truth of it; none of you. I have absolutely no picture of how you're made or what gives you satisfaction*' (ch. 26). When Oliver Lacon's wife Val, the 'child bride who had become a child mother', runs off with another man, the maudlin Lacon is bewildered: '"*We* were always taught that women had to be cherished. . . . If one didn't make 'em feel loved every minute of the day, they'd go off the rails"' (*SP*, ch. 20). Lizzie Worth, who passes from hand to hand in a game of marital and sexual pass-the-parcel, becomes in Jerry Westerby's romantic eyes the ultimate innocent victim, the one who pays the price. Lizzie's quixotic loyalties, and the horrors of her abuse at the hands of Drake Ko's enforcer, Tiu, make her an object of pity, but still an object. That is precisely the point. Le Carré's women are observed with increasing acuteness without ever being themselves more than persons who are acted upon. They are, in a sense, operational conveniences for the author.

Charlie in *The Little Drummer Girl* is a character of startling weakness and vulnerability. There is about her a 'central meekness', a too-ready submission to be the 'body-slave' of her lover Alastair; she fears ridicule, is inconsistent, superficial and half-educated. No wonder Martin Cruz Smith complained in *Esquire* that 'there remains a vacuum' at the centre of the novel. Other reviewers have found Charlie's motivation problematic and her conversion from aggressive radical to Israeli spy hard to accept. Charlie is the ultimate woman as object, the woman who is acted upon, but le Carré has taken the limitation of his characterization of women and transformed it into the impressive strength of this novel. He has portrayed in Charlie a quality of personality, an actress's plasticity of identity, which is (so far as one can tell) an absolutely central feature of the successful spy. As Alec Leamas lives his role so perfectly that it becomes his identity, so Charlie must, as Klaus Fuchs is reported to have said, live with a 'controlled schizophrenia'. The characters who lack this central plasticity, who are 'fixed' in their presence, are like Jerry Westerby and Jim Prideaux the naive and the deceived.

Charlie also embodies what Smiley and other Circus professionals feel about character and motivation. They are highly sceptical of agents who are too simply motivated, whether by anti-Communism or other causes, preferring a commitment made almost without positive content. In *The Looking-Glass War* this is called the 'second vow', made in the face of doubts and uncertainties. When Smiley thinks of Bill Haydon, the mysteriousness of the man's character reminds him of Russian dolls, one inside the other. (Churchill once described the USSR as a puzzle wrapped up in a mystery inside an enigma.) The political views of Charlie matter less to Kurtz than the chaotic forms of belief, the contradictions, ignorance and urgent seriousness of Charlie which might lend themselves to an epic performance in the 'theatre of the real'. It is the plasticity of structure he wants; the content can be dealt with in due course.

There are three 'families' in *The Little Drummer Girl*: the radical acting troupe, the Mossad team led by Kurtz and Becker and the Palestinian world of Khalil and his sister Fatmeh. Each offers to Charlie an identity, a place within, and a role to play in the real world designed to fill the nothingness which was her self-identity. Within the acting troupe Charlie is sometimes foundling and sometimes mother, 'the one who counted the money and knew where the anti-sting was, and the sticking-plaster for cut feet' (ch. 3). She is also their conscience, vigilant guard against chauvinist backsliding, and undisputed leading lady. The troupe is a family, living intensely within and keeping a clear gap between themselves and others. They 'name' people who catch their attention, and incorporate them very much on their own terms. If one declines to be 'pulled', either by the boys or girls, he becomes in Alastair's (dated?) accolade, 'cool'. Joseph's task, when he and Charlie meet on Mykonos, is to draw Charlie away from the family of actors. Himself playing the role of Joseph, the handsome lover, he gives her a role to play (the old impulsive, independent Charlie) when they land at Piraeus Harbour, and conveys her to the house where she will meet her new family.

Kurtz, as 'Marty', seeks at first to calm and reassure the furious actress by telling her she is among 'good people', 'decent people', 'non-sectarian, non-aligned, and deeply concerned like yourself about the many wrong directions the world is taking' (ch. 6). Kurtz clearly knows what he wants to do with Charlie:

> 'We are aiming to address the natural humanity in you, that is all. We are aiming at your good, caring, human heart. Your feelings. Your sense of right. We mean to ask nothing of you which conflicts in any wise with your strong and decent ethical concerns.' (ch.6)

He will play the role of the father Charlie never had, and flatter the virtuous daughter in her: 'He had granted her an early glimpse of the new family she might care to join, knowing that deep down, like most rebels, she was only looking for a better conformity' (ch. 6). Layers of pose, self-delusion and deceit are stripped away, leaving Charlie utterly in the hands of the Israelis:

> their action, their abstemiousness, their clear-eyed zeal, their authenticity, their true allegiance . . . fill[ed] the emptiness that had yawned and screamed inside her like a bored demon ever since she could remember. (ch. 7)

They offer Charlie a new role in the 'theatre', a family and something else: 'Thank God, she thought: a homeland at last'.

Kurtz, however, wants a volunteer not a coerced psychological wreck, and advises Becker to keep his distance from Charlie. But the logic of the fiction they proceed to create, the 'new reality' of Charlie's relationship with Michel, draws them into a dizzyingly complex relationship. Gadi Becker plays

Joseph, and assists in the process by which Charlie's feelings about Joseph inevitably are transferred to the imaginary Michel they are creating: she loves Joseph as Michel, and Joseph as himself. Each offers Charlie a purpose, an identity, which she must master and sustain. As Joseph he initiates her into the role she must play; as Michel he brings her towards joining the 'secret army' of Khalil and becoming a 'little soldier' in the Palestinian cause.

Charlie stands at the centre of the drama, but a parallel struggle takes place within Joseph. We have brief glimpses of his unease at the role which he finds himself playing, and of his doubts at the efficacy of the 'cords of discipline' which govern his professional life. There is a very revealing moment when Charlie asks Joseph what he fought for: ' "In '56 because I wanted to be a hero, in '67 for peace. And in '73" – he seemed to find it harder to remember – "for Israel".' (*LDG*, ch. 12). The slight pause betrays a deeper uncertainty of purpose, and an inner link with Smiley (who ends *Smiley's People* in a similar state of mind). It is only with 'the hardness of a willed allegiance' that he accepts the logic behind the murder of the Dutch 'comfort girl' along with Michel. But, like Smiley, accept he does in the end. Joseph is a complex and paradoxical character: he must be sexually magnetic, and yet maintain sufficient distance between himself and Charlie to sustain the fiction they create; between them is a 'shared schizophrenia'. Where Charlie is chaotic, explosively voluble and confused, Joseph is calm, orderly and exudes certainty. He withholds himself from her, and from the narration, as Charlie yields herself up utterly.

When Charlie goes 'below the line' and is interrogated by Khalil (unnamed) she is reassured that her questioners are 'nice' and 'reasonable'. 'We're committed people but we are not psychopaths' (ch. 20). The brevity of the scene is enough: it is a replay of the earlier interrogation of Charlie by Kurtz, and a prelude to her admission to the Palestinian family. The next chapter begins with their arrival in Beirut. After questioning by Captain Tayeh, Charlie is taken south, towards the Palestinian camps near Sidon. The reality of conditions in the Lebanon impose themselves upon her as a further stage in an education:

She was a blinkered rider, being conveyed through events and emotions too great for her to encompass into a land where merely to be present was to be part of a monstrous injustice. She had joined the victims and was finally reconciled to her deceit. (*LDG*, ch. 21)

Fatmeh welcomes Charlie as a sister. Khalil addresses her in similar terms:

'You are one of us. You are our sister. Fatmeh says you are our sister. You have no home, but you are part of a great family. We can make you a new identity, or you can go to Fatmeh, live with her as long as you wish.' (ch. 26)

The image of Fatmeh swabbing the eyes of a baby makes Charlie yearn for a similar role, to help Fatmeh 'for the rest of her life'. In the hillside training camp Charlie experiences a sympathy that had previously been denied her. The description of the march and procession which ends in the terror of an Israeli air raid is written with a disciplined anger. Charlie's conversion is *earned* within the novel; '*The only loyalty is to be here*'.

The politics of *The Little Drummer Girl* are not to be settled by a balancing of political opinions within the text, by a measuring of one 'monstrous injustice' against another. Such matters should not be settled by opinions, but by the way political meaning is enacted in the novel. We are carefully shown how Charlie's radicalism is discredited by her own inadequacies; how the casuistry of Kurtz qualifies his relationship to Zionism, as does the ambiguity of Becker; the nature of the tensions within the Israeli 'family' over the correct response to Palestinian terrorism; and, ultimately, our reading of the book's politics is coloured by the perception readers make of the justice of the Palestinian cause, and the discrepancy between the ends of the movement and the terroristic means. The discrepancy between ends and means on the Israeli side raises the same problems. The Palestinian case appears here in damaged forms, through the vicious western sympathizers (Helga, Rossino, Mesterbein); it is in the portrayal of the Palestinians that le Carré's grasp of the dignity of their cause, and its ruthlessness, is most evident. They are not evil, though they do many evil things. Such a notion arouses the deepest anxieties in friends of Israel, and has resulted in some extraordinarily tortured accusations of pro-Arab propaganda on le Carré's part. The proposition which has given deepest offence to Zionist critics ('The Zionists kill for fear and for hate . . . Palestinians for love and justice') seems to me an entirely reasonable distinction for a *Palestinian* to make. The chilling portrait of Khalil, who says he kills for love, 'for Palestine and for her children', and who makes a little dolly out of spare detonator wire, is not calculated to win friends in the west for the Palestinian cause. The notion, canvassed by William Buckley, Jr, in the *New York Times Book Review*, that le Carré 'permits the Palestinian point to be made with rare and convincing eloquence' demonstrates, if proof were needed, that the 'Palestinian point' is made only within the assumptions of the west. That is to say, it is not made at all, or at least not as Palestinians would care to have their experience articulated.

When le Carré visited the headquarters of the exiled Palestinians in Tunis in 1983 he expressed sympathy not for the PLO but for the ordinary Palestinians who were left behind to bear the consequences of Israeli reprisals for acts of PLO terrorism: sympathy not for a cause, but for people caught in an historical tragedy. While in Tunis he met a Palestinian named Faisal who had served as the bodyguard and security officer of Ali Hassan Salameh, who was blown up by a car bomb in 1979. (The names *Fatmeh* and *Khalil* were drawn from Faisal's wife and his younger son.) Le Carré based Khalil upon the description he received from Faisal of this dead terrorist: Salameh, he wrote in the *Observer* in 1983,

> was one of the most enigmatic and conspiratorial figures in the PLO. He was the son of a foremost Palestinian leader who was killed in the war of '48. Arafat called him his lion. The Israelis had no such admiration for him and wanted him dead for his part in the 1972 Munich massacre. . . . But the Israelis had another reason to kill Salameh, for, as the *Wall Street Journal* recently reported, he seems to have been the Americans' principal operational link with the PLO, the man

who helped implement the understanding that Arafat's Fatah would not harm American personnel. He also helped line up the American evacuation from Beirut in the civil war of '75/'76.

On the other hand, to assert that the book is either Zionist or imperialist is profoundly mistaken. The political 'balance' in the book is not in fact sustained; the book does take sides. But it does not endorse either of the sides which are so violently in contention. He gives the book a surprising romantic ending; this is the *side* he is on. (Le Carré is more romantic than many readers have understood. How else could he have imagined a Jerry Westerby?) Love may not, in the real world, conquer all, but as Irina scribbled in her diary 'we have only to open the door and step outside to be free' (*TTSS*, ch. 8).

*

Le Carré's critics have not found a handy phrase like 'Greeneland' to describe the dour and pessimistic landscape of his fictions, but complaints along that line have often been expressed, and even by critics as well disposed to le Carré as Tom Paulin: 'Le Carré's imagination', he wrote in a review of *Smiley's People* in *Encounter*, 'has a quiet brooding heroic quality of reined-in bitterness'. There is a vein of romanticism in le Carré, already noted; a stinging satirical touch which is unmercifully let loose on a character like Oliver Lacon; and there is also a distinct vein of comedy – black comedy – which has strengthened in his books of the past dozen years. The dark horror of the death of Otto Leipzig (*SP*, ch. 17) is preceded by a comic moment in which Smiley asks a young couple, momentarily interrupted from their lovemaking, about Otto's whereabouts. In the water camp a glimpse occurs into the heart of our own particular darkness: not just the brutal murder in the *Isadora*, but the casual violence and menace of the young men who surround Smiley's car: 'Smiley looked at the boy's face and saw no human instinct that he understood'. (The idea of the 'human bond', and the just fate of those who break it, is central to the ethical dilemmas posed by Kurtz in *The Little Drummer Girl*.) But in Ostrakova, perhaps, and Toby

98

Esterhase in *Smiley's People*, we see essentially comic modes of characterization at work, and in *A Perfect Spy* le Carré has created his first major comic character, Rick Pym. (Old Hugo, Aldo's father in *The Naive and Sentimental Lover*, is a sketch for the full-blown Rick Pym.) The novel comes alive when he is allowed the centre stage of his son Magnus's recollections. The novel might easily be subtitled *The Joy of Spying*, so far has it moved from the 'reined-in bitterness' of le Carré's earlier books.

It is written in the form of an extended suicide note from Magnus Pym, British diplomat, station head of the Secret Intelligence Service (MI6) in Vienna and long-time Czech mole in British intelligence. After coming back to England to attend the funeral of his father, Pym disappears to a safe house he has prepared years before. His British colleagues desperately try to locate him (another defector would seriously weaken the 'special relationship' in intelligence) and to hide his absence from the already suspicious CIA. At one level the narrative describes the efforts of Jack Brotherhood, a senior officer in the Firm, the man who recruited Pym and guided his career, to track down the person who has betrayed him. At the same time, through Pym's digressive and detailed letter to his son Tom (another narrative technique tentatively introduced in *The Naive and Sentimental Lover*), scene after scene of Magnus's childhood, his experiences at school, in the Army, at Oxford and in British intelligence are portrayed. Each chapter carries the narrative forward in real time, while probing ever deeper into Pym's background and early life.

The inner structure of *A Perfect Spy* is similar to that of *The Little Drummer Girl*, in which Charlie, a central nothingness, stands in relationship to three 'families' who create and possess her. In *A Perfect Spy* the relationships have a different shape:

Rick Pym
('his one true anchor')
$\downarrow$

Axel $\longrightarrow$ Magnus $\longleftarrow$ Jack Brotherhood
(the two 'saints' he has loved and betrayed)

Like Charlie, Magnus is an absence, someone who tries always to please, to make people happy, to – in his father's idiom – see them right. He is surrounded by 'parents' who own him, keep him going. 'Both [Axel and Brotherhood] admired him, both loved his jokes and his voices, both were ready to occupy the empty spaces of his heart. In return he was giving to each man the character he seemed to be in search of' (*PS*, ch. 8). Brotherhood 'invents' Magnus as a spy in Berne, by persuading the willing young man to write reports on student politics, and he follows Magnus's career, easing his path into high responsibility within the Firm, defending him against American suspicions until the last moment, and then pursuing Magnus with a determination only given to those who have been bitterly betrayed. Brotherhood even allows Magnus free rein with his lover, Mary, a 'top Martha' in the Firm. It is the successful marriage with Mary which ensures Magnus's posting to the USA, the golden land of opportunity for spies. Brotherhood gives up Mary, but still holds her love, as he holds Magnus: 'It was Pym's soul you were after, not the piffling translation' (*PS*, ch. 8) he has sent him for in Berne.

Magnus meets Axel in Berne on the same day that he is recruited by Brotherhood, and their relationship becomes the single most important one in his adult life: 'Axel was his keeper and his virtue, he was the altar on which Pym had laid his secrets and his life. He had become the part of Pym that was not owned by anybody else' (ch. 7). Magnus betrays Axel, almost as an act of kindness to Brotherhood. As an illegal alien in Switzerland Axel is arrested and expelled to Czechoslovakia. It is not Magnus's first betrayal, for he had done a similar act to his friend Sefton Boyd, but it leaves a deep mark on the young man's conscience. Their paths cross again while Magnus is serving in the Intelligence Corps in Austria and Axel is working for Czech intelligence. The resulting agreement they arrive at, their separate peace, transforms Magnus into an upwardly mobile double agent. The relationship between the two is based on love and trust; they create a 'middle ground' of affection which le Carré portrays in comic Forsterian terms:

[Pym] would never again betray his friend for the illusion of being a servant of national necessity. His loves, his duties and allegiances had never been clearer. Axel, I owe you. Together we can change the world. I will bring you gifts as you brought gifts to me. I will never again send you to the camps. (ch. 8)

Le Carré has never before written with such gaiety about the joys of spying, the triumphs stolen from the powers and bureaucracies and the shared intimacy of secrecy; he has never perhaps revealed so clearly the vein of anti-establishment feeling within himself. Between Axel and Magnus there is no mutuality. After betraying Axel in Switzerland, Magnus spent the rest of his life trying to put right the wrong he had done. Axel becomes more than a friend, he is a confessor, and the 'wise and steady father Pym had never had' (ch. 16); once Magnus takes his second vow there is no turning back. It is Axel who gives him Sabina, his first lover, while he was serving in Austria, as well as the copy of *Simplicissimus*, the seventeenth-century German picaresque account of the Thirty Years War, which formed the basis of their coded communications. (Is this the same copy of Grimmelshausen which Smiley leaves at Roddy Martindale's club in the second chapter of *Tinker, Tailor*?) He is 'source Greensleeves' for Magnus in Austria, and after Magnus was posted to the USA Axel happily followed. When the Americans begin to draw conclusions from certain coincidences relating to Czech broadcasts and Magnus's presence in the USA, Axel begs Magnus to break off his work and save himself. When Magnus disappears Axel desperately seeks to find him, and to offer a safe haven in Czechoslovakia for his erring agent and friend. It is an offer he knows would not interest Magnus, but it was made out of love and concern, and also out of an apprehension that his friend would prefer suicide to the life of a defector if caught out.

The third corner of the triangle controlling Magnus is his father, Rick, a con-man *par excellence*. The novel is dedicated to 'R.C.' (Ronnie Cornwell) and after the author's discussion in the *Sunday Times* of his relations with his father, Rick Pym inevitably takes on a heightened importance. He, more than

Axel and Brotherhood, claims possession of Magnus. Every step in his son's life is part of Rick's grand vision of doing right by everybody, and getting rich in the process. 'You wanted my living spirit to enter your dying body and give you back the life I owed you' (*PS*, ch. 6). He adores Magnus and sends him cheques which bounce; he plans a great future for him in the law, while involving him in terrible frauds and deceptions. He sends bribes to the wrong professors at Oxford and fails to pay Magnus's school fees. Rick's court includes the one person to whom Magnus gives uncompromised love (the Jewish refugee Lippsie, one of Rick's 'Lovelies' who becomes Magnus's tutor: she is the third woman to pass from the hands of his 'father's' to his own). Rick's mysterious dealings, his unexplained absences and requests to hide things, his wickedly comic political career as a Liberal candidate and his undoing by Mrs Wentworth, the widow of a man whom Rick bilked out of thousands of pounds, weigh upon Magnus and teach him stealth, subterfuge, dissimulation and tradecraft. He learns to seek out innocuous legitimacy, to value secrets as an inflation-free currency and instrument of power at first in the act of spying upon his father, and then as a general rule of conduct: 'his strategy was to pacify and reconcile, and keep all the threads in his own hands' (*PS*, ch. 6).

In trying to please and love everyone, Magnus betrays them all. He evades Rick and lies to him; he turns Axel over to the British in Switzerland and later thinks seriously about betraying him to the CIA to save himself, and in the end simply walks out on him; he betrays Jack Brotherhood from the first. He betrays his schoolmate Sefton Boyd, his two wives, Belinda and Mary, his country, his service, his colleagues and the 'loquacious and disarming' Americans. Yet Magnus is not an ideological traitor. The hints in the book of his political views (mainly reverence of Uncle Joe Stalin) simply reinforce the personal roots of his actions. As Sefton Boyd put it: '"Didn't care about money. Love was all he cared about"' (*PS*, ch. 12). Betrayal and duplicity only mean choosing who you hope to see right:

Betrayal as hope and compensation. (ch. 5)

> Love is whatever you can still betray, he thought. Betrayal can only happen if you love. (ch. 10)

Magnus is a very hopeful, a very loving man.

*A Perfect Spy* is the most autobiographical of le Carré's books. The Pym family background in Poole, the Nonconformist piety and repression of a childhood, the absent mother and scapegrace father, the public school, Army Intelligence Corps and Oxford experience belong as well to the biography of David Cornwell as to Magnus Pym. He seems, at mid-career, to have opened a new door.

In a review in the *New York Times Book Review* of *The Honourable Schoolboy* the novelist Anthony Burgess asks an uncomfortable question about le Carré, and provides a thoroughly negative answer:

> Does [this book] have anything to do with literature? In the sense that literature is recognizable through its capacity to evoke more than it says, is based on artful selection, throws up symbols, suggests a theology or metaphysic of which the story itself is a kind of allegory, the answer has to be no.

Returning to le Carré nine years later, in a review of *A Perfect Spy* for the *Observer*, Burgess is quicker to grant at least some merit: 'Mr le Carré's talents cry out to be employed in the creation of a real novel'. While grudgingly allowing that *A Perfect Spy* has 'the appearance of the difficulty of real literature', Burgess's point is that no matter how well done, the spy thriller is still 'sub-art'. It seems to me on both these central issues Burgess is simply wrong. I have argued here, as indeed have others, that a tradition of writing (initiated by Somerset Maugham) emerges in the 1920s as a critique of and divagation from the Buchanesque thriller. It is this change, and also the political climate of the 1930s, which opens the way for Eric Ambler and Graham Greene and, a generation later, for le Carré. What this process involves is the creation of a space for 'real literature' within the formula genre of the spy thriller. For writers like Oppenheim and 'Sapper' the formula was everything. Ambler and Greene showed how comprehensively the formulae and politics of the spy thriller could be altered. For

John le Carré the formulae of the spy thriller are little more than mild pretexts for profound and fully serious investigations of the central issues of our time. Le Carré *uses* the spy thriller to write 'real' novels. Critics who study the forms of the spy thriller (like Bruce Merry) are often faintly disappointed at how little the books of le Carré fit into the formula genre. Turning that point around, as I have tried to do here, reading le Carré as a novelist is a singularly rewarding business. He consistently evokes large social dilemmas; his books use symbols (is not the dilapidated Circus the most resonant symbol in our time for the state of England?); the author of *The Spy Who Came in From the Cold* and *Tinker, Tailor, Soldier, Spy* has no cause to apologize for the powers of literary construction displayed in his books; and, above all, the novels of le Carré imply not so much a theology or a metaphysic but an ethics of the way we live now.

# BIBLIOGRAPHY

## WORKS BY JOHN LE CARRÉ

*Novels*

*Call for the Dead.* London: Gollancz, 1961. New York: Walker, 1962. Harmondsworth: Penguin, 1964 (as *The Deadly Affair*).
   Review: *New York Times Book Review*, 7 April 1963 (Anthony Boucher).
*A Murder of Quality.* London: Gollancz, 1962. New York: Walker, 1963.
   Review: *The Times Literary Supplement*, 31 August 1962.
*The Spy Who Came in From the Cold.* London: Gollancz, 1963. New York: Coward-McCann, 1964.
   Reviews: *The Times*, 12 September 1963; *Daily Mail*, 12 September 1963 (Kenneth Allsop); *The Times Literary Supplement*, 13 September 1963; *Sunday Times*, 15 September 1963 (Robert Harling); *Observer*, 15 September 1963 (Maurice Richardson); *Guardian*, 11 October 1963 (Francis Iles); *New York Times Book Review*, 12 January 1964 (Anthony Boucher); *New York Review of Books*, 5 March 1964 (Robert M. Adams); *Atlantic Monthly*, May 1964 (William Barrett).
*The Le Carré Omnibus (Call for the Dead, A Murder of Quality).* London: Gollancz, 1964. New York: Walker, 1964 (as *The Incongruous Spy: Two Novels of Suspense*).
*The Looking-Glass War.* London: Heinemann, 1965. New York: Coward-McCann, 1965.
   Reviews: *The Times Literary Supplement*, 24 June 1965; *The Times*, 24 June 1965; *Saturday Review*, 24 July 1965 (Granville Hicks); *Book Week*, 25 July 1965 (J. K. Galbraith); *New York Times Book Review*, 25 July 1965 (George P. Elliott); *New York Review of Books*, 5 August 1965 (Steven Marcus); *Atlantic Monthly*, August 1965 (William Barrett).
*A Small Town in Germany.* London: Heinemann, 1968. New York: Coward-McCann, 1968.

Reviews: *Book World*, 20 October 1968 (Malcolm Muggeridge); *New York Times Book Review*, 27 October 1968 (Richard Boston); *New Statesman*, 8 November 1968 (T. G. Rosenthal); *National Review*, 19 November 1968 (Guy Davenport).

*The Naive and Sentimental Lover*. London: Hodder & Stoughton, 1971. New York: Alfred A. Knopf, 1971.

Reviews: *Sunday Express*, 19 September 1971 (Graham Lord); *The Times Literary Supplement*, 24 September 1971; *Spectator*, 25 September 1971 (Auberon Waugh); *Observer*, 26 September 1971 (Claire Tomalin); *Sunday Times*, 26 September 1971 (Frederic Raphael).

*Tinker, Tailor, Soldier, Spy*. New York: Alfred A. Knopf, 1974. London: Hodder & Stoughton, 1974.

Reviews: *New Leader*, 24 June 1974 (Pearl K. Bell); *Listener*, 4 July 1974 (Derek Mahon); *New Statesman*, 12 July 1974 (Timothy Mo); *The Times Literary Supplement*, 19 July 1974.

*The Honourable Schoolboy*. London: Hodder & Stoughton, 1977. New York: Alfred A. Knopf, 1977.

Reviews: *The Times*, 8 September 1977 (H. R. F. Keating); *Guardian*, 8 September 1977 (Clancy Sigal); *The Times Literary Supplement*, 9 September 1977 (T. J. Binyon); *Observer*, 11 September 1977 (Maurice Richardson), *Sunday Times*, 11 September 1977 (Edmund Crispin); *New York Times*, 22 September 1977 (John Leonard); *New York Times Book Review*, 25 September 1977 (Anthony Burgess); *New York Review of Books*, 27 October 1977 (Clive James); *New Review*, October 1977 (James Fenton).

*Smiley's People*. Franklin Center, Pa: Franklin Library, 1979. (First limited edn, with illustrations by Ben F. Wohlberg.) New York: Alfred A. Knopf, 1980. London: Hodder & Stoughton, 1980.

Reviews: *New York Times Book Review*, 6 January 1980 (Michael Wood); *New Republic*, 5–12 January 1980 (Julian Moynahan); *Observer*, 3 February 1980 (A. Alvarez); *New York Review of Books*, 7 February 1980 (V. S. Pritchett); *New Statesman*, 8 February 1980 (David Caute); *The Times Literary Supplement*, 8 February 1980 (S. S. Prawer); *Encounter*, June 1980 (Tom Paulin).

*The Spy Who Came in From the Cold, Call for the Dead, A Murder of Quality, The Looking-Glass War, A Small Town in Germany*. London: Heinemann and Octopus Books, 1979.

*The Quest for Karla* (*Tinker, Tailor, Soldier, Spy, The Honourable Schoolboy, Smiley's People*). New York: Alfred A. Knopf, 1982. London: Hodder & Stoughton, 1982.

*The Little Drummer Girl*. New York: Alfred A. Knopf, 1983. London: Hodder & Stoughton, 1983.

Reviews: *New York Times Book Review*, 13 March 1983 (William F. Buckley, Jr); *The Times Literary Supplement*, 25 March 1983

(T. J. Binyon); *Sunday Times*, 27 March 1983 (Julian Symons); *Observer*, 27 March 1983 (John Gross); *Daily Mail*, 31 March 1983 (Auberon Waugh); *The Times*, 31 March 1983 (Anthony Quinton); *Jewish Chronicle*, 1 April 1983 (Gerald Kaufman, MP); *Spectator*, 2 April 1983 (Andrew Boyle); *Esquire*, April 1983 (Martin Cruz Smith); *Tribune*, 8 April 1983 (Chris Mullin); *New York Review of Books*, 14 April 1983 (James Wolcott); *New Republic*, 18 April 1983 (David Pryce-Jones); *Commentary*, June 1983 (Walter Laqueur); *Encounter*, July 1983 (Clive Sinclair); *Literary Review*, July 1983 (Christopher Hitchins).

*A Perfect Spy*. London: Hodder & Stoughton, 1986. New York: Alfred A. Knopf, 1986.

Reviews: *Observer*, 16 March 1986 (Anthony Burgess); *Sunday Express*, 16 March 1986 (Graham Lord); *The Times*, 20 March 1986 (Tim Heald); *Guardian*, 20 March 1986 (Julian Symons); *Daily Telegraph*, 21 March 1986; *New York Review of Books*, 29 May 1986 (Noel Annan).


## Short fiction

'Dare I Weep, Dare I Mourn'. *Saturday Evening Post*, 28 January 1967.

'What Ritual Is Being Observed Tonight?' *Saturday Evening Post*, 2 November 1968.


## Non-fiction

'The Writer and the Spy'. *Daily Telegraph*, 29 March 1964.

'To Russia with Greetings: An Open Letter to the Moscow *Literary Gazette*'. *Encounter*, May 1966.

'The Spy to End Spies'. *Encounter*, November 1966 (on Richard Sorge).

'What Every Writer Wants'. *Cornhill*, Winter 1966–7.

'Introduction'. In Bruce Page, David Leitch and Phillip Knightley, *Philby: The Spy who Betrayed a Generation*. London: André Deutsch, 1968.

'Vocation in a World of Pain'. *Sunday Times*, 25 October 1970 (on C. P. Snow).

'Well played, Wodehouse'. *Sunday Times*, 10 October 1971.

'In a Small Place in Cornwall'. *Sunday Telegraph Magazine*, 6 September 1974 (on the painter Kurt Weschke).

Biographical statement. In John Wakeman (ed.), *World Authors 1950–1970*, pp. 841–2. New York: H. W. Wilson, 1975.

'England Made Me'. *Observer*, 13 November 1977.

Book-of-the-year choice. *Sunday Times*, 4 December 1977 (Marquez,

The Autumn of the Patriarch; Pritchett, The Gentle Barbarian; Herr, Dispatches).

'An American Spy Story'. New York Times Book Review, 14 October 1979 (review of Thomas Powers, The Man Who Kept the Secrets: Richard Helms and the CIA).

'At Last, It's Smiley'. Sunday Telegraph Magazine, 21 October 1979.

'Siege'. Observer, 1 June 1980.

'McCullin's World'. Sunday Times Magazine, 26 October 1980. Reprinted as an introduction to Hearts of Darkness: Photographs by Don McCullin. London: Secker & Warburg, 1980.

'Unlicensed to Quote'. The Times, 17 March 1981 (letter on Sir Maurice Oldfield).

Review of Piers Paul Read, The Villa Golitsyn. The Times, 8 October 1981.

'Memories of a Vanished Land'. Observer, 13 June 1982.

'Exiles in the White Hotel'. Observer, 26 June 1983.

'Tribute to Richard Hughes'. The Times, 5 January 1985.

'Spying on my Father'. Sunday Times, 16 March 1986.

'Don't be Beastly to your Secret Service'. Sunday Times, 23 March 1986.


*Interviews*

Jordan Bonfante, Life, 28 February 1964.

'Atticus', Sunday Times, 21 June 1964.

Robert Pitman, Sunday Express, 14 February 1965.

'Atticus', Sunday Times, 20 June 1965.

Michael Dornan, Western Daily Press and Bristol Mirror, 21 June 1965.

Anthea Goddard, Glasgow Evening Times, 21 June 1965.

Véra Volmane, Les Nouvelles Littéraires, 23 September 1965.

Leigh Crutchley, Listener, 14 April 1966.

Alan Watson, Sunday Times, 30 March 1969.

Michael Dean, Listener, 5 September 1974.

James Cameron, New York Times Magazine, 8 September 1974.

Melvyn Bragg, Listener, 22 January 1976.

'Heathman', Hampstead and Highgate Express, 9 September 1977.

Philip Oakes, Sunday Times, 11 September 1977.

Tim Heald, Radio Times, 22 September 1977.

Michael Barber, New York Times Book Review, 25 September 1977.

Paul Vaughan, Listener, 13 September 1979.

Miriam Gross, Observer, 3 February 1982.

Nicholas Wapshott, The Times, 6 September 1982.

Byron Rogers, Radio Times, 18–24 September 1982.

Melvyn Bragg, New York Times Book Review, 13 March 1983.

Edward Behr, Hampstead and Highgate Express, 25 March 1983.

Joseph Lelyveld, New York Times Magazine, 16 March 1986.

*Films based on the novels of John le Carré*

*The Spy Who Came in From the Cold*, dir. Martin Ritt. Screenplay by Paul Dehn and Guy Trosper. Salem Productions, 1965.

*The Deadly Affair*, dir. Sydney Lumet. Screenplay by Paul Dehn. Sydney Lumet Productions, 1966.

*The Looking-Glass War*, dir. Frank R. Pierson. Screenplay by Frank R. Pierson. Columbia Pictures, 1969.

*Tinker, Tailor, Soldier, Spy*, dir. John Irvin. Screenplay by Arthur Hopcraft. BBC/Paramount Pictures, 1979.

*Smiley's People*, dir. Simon Langton. Screenplay by John le Carré and John Hopkin. BBC/Paramount Pictures, 1981.

*The Little Drummer Girl*, dir. George Roy Hill. Screenplay by Loring Mandel. Warner Brothers, 1984.

## CRITICAL AND HISTORICAL

*Books*

Ambler, Eric. *Background to Danger*. London: Hodder & Stoughton, 1937.

—— *Here Lies: An Autobiography*. London: Weidenfeld & Nicolson, 1985.

Andrew, Christopher. *Secret Service: The Making of the British Intelligence Community*. London: Heinemann, 1985.

Atkins, John. *The British Spy Novel: Styles in Treachery*. London: John Calder, 1984.

Barley, Tony. *Taking Sides: The Fiction of John le Carré*. Milton Keynes: Open University Press, 1986.

Bradbury, Malcolm. *The Social Context of Modern English Literature*. Oxford: Blackwell, 1971.

Buchan, John. *The Thirty Nine Steps*. Edinburgh: Blackwood, 1915.

Cawelti, John G. *Adventure, Mystery and Romance: Formula Stories as Art and Popular Culture*. Chicago: University of Chicago Press, 1976.

Childers, Erskine. *The Riddle of the Sands*. London: Sidgwick & Jackson, 1903.

Curtis, Anthony. *The Pattern of Maugham*. London: Hamish Hamilton, 1974.

Deacon, Richard. *'C': A Biography of Sir Maurice Oldfield*. London: Macdonald, 1984.

del Buono, Oreste and Eco, Umberto (eds). *The Bond Affair*. London: Macdonald, 1966.

Driberg, Tom. *Guy Burgess: A Portrait with Background*. London: Weidenfeld & Nicolson, 1956.

Fleming, Ian. *Casino Royale*. London: Cape, 1953.

Forster, E. M. *Two Cheers for Democracy*. London: Edward Arnold, 1951.

Garnett, David (ed.). *The Letters of T. E. Lawrence*. London: Cape, 1938.

Greene, Graham. *Stamboul Train*. London: Heinemann, 1932.

—— *Ways of Escape*. London: Bodley Head, 1980.

Harper, Ralph. *The World of the Thriller*. Cleveland, Ohio: Case Western Reserve University Press, 1969.

Hoggart, Richard. *The Uses of Literacy*. London: Chatto & Windus, 1957.

Kennaway, James. *Some Gorgeous Accident: A Novel*. London: Longmans Green, 1967.

—— and Kennaway, Susan. *The Kennaway Papers*. London: Cape, 1981.

Leavis, F. R. *Mass Civilization and Minority Culture*. Cambridge: Gordon Fraser, 1930.

Lonsdale, Gordon. *Spy: Twenty Years of Secret Service*. London: Neville Spearman, 1965.

Masters, Anthony. *The Man Who Was M: The Life of Maxwell Knight*. Oxford: Blackwell, 1984.

Maugham, W. Somerset. *Ashenden, or: The British Agent*. London: Heinemann, 1928.

Merry, Bruce. *Anatomy of the Spy Thriller*. Dublin: Gill & Macmillan, 1977.

Monaghan, David. *The Novels of John le Carré*. Oxford: Blackwell, 1985.

Morgan, Ted. *Somerset Maugham*. London: Cape, 1980.

Page, Bruce, Leitch, David and Knightley, Phillip. *Philby: The Spy who Betrayed a Generation*. London: André Deutsch, 1968.

Palmer, Jerry. *Thrillers: Genesis and Structure of a Popular Genre*. London: Edward Arnold, 1978.

Panek, LeRoy L. *The Special Branch: The British Spy Novel, 1890–1980*. Bowling Green, Ky: Bowling Green University Popular Press, 1981.

Pearson, John. *The Life of Ian Fleming*. New York: McGraw-Hill, 1966.

Philby, Eleanor. *Kim Philby: The Spy I Loved*. London: Hamish Hamilton, 1968.

Philby, Kim. *My Silent War*, with an Introduction by Graham Greene. London: MacGibbon & Kee, 1968.

Powers, Thomas. *The Man Who Kept the Secrets: Richard Helms and the CIA*. London: Weidenfeld & Nicolson, 1980.

Rockwell, R. Joan. *Fact in Fiction*. London: Routledge & Kegan Paul, 1974.

Rutherford, Andrew. *The Literature of War: Five Studies in Heroic Virtue*. London: Macmillan, 1978.

Sauerberg, Lars Ole. *Secret Agents in Fiction: Ian Fleming, John le Carré and Len Deighton*. London: Macmillan, 1984.

Straight, Michael. *After Long Silence*. New York: W. W. Norton, 1983.

Sutherland, John. *Bestsellers: Popular Fiction of the 1970s*. London: Routledge & Kegan Paul, 1981.

Symons, Julian. *Bloody Murder: From the Detective Story to the Crime Novel*. London: Faber & Faber, 1972; rev. edn Harmondsworth: Penguin, 1974.


*Articles*

Anon. 'Cloak without Dagger'. *The Times Literary Supplement*, 8 February 1963, p. 29.

Anon. 'I Spy with my Little Eye'. *The Economist*, 4 January 1975, pp. 81–3.

Barzun, Jacques. 'Meditations on the Literature of Spying'. *American Scholar*, 34 (1965), pp. 167–78.

Cook, Bruce. 'Cold War Fiction'. *Commonweal*, 83 (17 December 1965), pp. 342–5.

Davis, Curtis. 'Speak to Me Softly: The Permanent Fascination of the Spy Story'. *Columbia University Forum*, 4 (Spring 1961), pp. 26–30.

—— 'The Figure Behind the Landscape: The Emergence of the Secret Agent in British Belles-Lettres'. *Southern Humanities Review*, 1 (1967), pp. 223–35.

Foot, M. R. D. 'Open Secrets'. *The Economist*, 15 March 1980, pp. 51–4, 56–8.

Freeling, Nicolas. 'Crime Novels'. *The Times Literary Supplement*, 24 June 1965, p. 539.

French, David. 'Spy Fever in Britain 1900–1915'. *Historical Journal*, 21 (1978), pp. 355–70.

Gardner, John. 'The Espionage Novel'. In H. R. F. Keating (ed.), *Whodunnit? A Guide to Crime, Suspense and Spy Fiction*. London: Windward, 1982.

Gillespie, Robert. 'The Recent Future: Secret Agents and the Cold War'. *Salmagundi*, Summer 1970, pp. 45–60.

Grella, George. 'John le Carré: Murder and Loyalty'. *New Republic*, 31 July 1976, pp. 23–5.

Halperin, John. 'Between Two Worlds: The Novels of John le Carré'. *South Atlantic Quarterly*, 79 (1980), pp. 17–37.

Hopcraft, Arthur. 'How Smiley Came to Life: John le Carré Traces the History of Alec Guiness's Television Role'. *Sunday Telegraph Magazine*, 21 October 1977.

Hughes, Celia. 'Serious Reflections on Light Reading: the World of John le Carré'. *Theology*, 84 (July 1981), pp. 274–9.

Kanfer, Stefan. 'The Spy Who Came in for the Gold'. *Time Magazine*, 3 October 1977.

Kennedy, Paul. 'Riddle of the Sands'. *The Times*, 3 January 1981, p. 7.

Knightley, Phillip. 'Dinner with the Spymaster'. *Sunday Times*, 15 March 1981, p. 13 (interview with Sir Maurice Oldfield).

Monaghan, David. 'John le Carré and England: A Spy's-Eye View'. *Modern Fiction Studies*, 29 (Autumn, 1983), pp. 569–82.

Most, Glenn W. 'The Hippocratic Smile: John le Carré and the Traditions of the Detective Novel'. In Glenn W. Most and William W. Stowe (eds), *The Poetics of Murder: Detective Fiction and Literary Theory*, pp. 341–65. New York: Harcourt Brace Jovanovich, 1983.

Neuse, Steven M. 'Bureaucratic Malaise in the Modern Spy Novel: Deighton, Greene and le Carré'. *Public Administration*, 60 (Autumn 1982), pp. 293–306.

Palmer, Jerry. 'Thrillers: The Deviant Behind the Consensus'. In Ian Taylor and Laurie Taylor (eds), *Politics and Deviance*, pp. 136–56. Harmondsworth: Pelican, 1973.

—— 'The Thriller'. In H. R. F. Keating (ed.), *Whodunnit? A Guide to Crime, Suspense and Spy Fiction*, pp. 61–4. London: Windward, 1982.

——'Thrillers'. In Christopher Pawling (ed.), *Popular Fiction and Social Change*, pp. 76–98. London: Macmillan, 1984.

Rothberg, Abraham. 'The Decline and Fall of George Smiley: John le Carré and English Decency'. *Southwest Review*, 66 (Autumn 1981), pp. 377–93.

Stafford, David. 'Spies and Gentlemen: The Birth of the British Spy Novel, 1893–1914'. *Victorian Studies*, 24 (Summer 1981), pp. 489–509.

Usborne, Richard. 'Spies Brought to Book'. *London Magazine*, n.s. 8, 2 (May 1968), pp. 53–60; 9 (December 1968), pp. 85–90.